The Little Guide to Writing for Impact

The Little Guide to Writing for Impact

How to Communicate Research in a Way That People Will Read

Katherine Barrett, Richard Greene, and Donald F. Kettl

ROWMAN & LITTLEFIELD
Lanham • Boulder • New York • London

Published by Rowman & Littlefield
An imprint of The Rowman & Littlefield Publishing Group, Inc.
4501 Forbes Boulevard, Suite 200, Lanham, Maryland 20706
www.rowman.com

86-90 Paul Street, London EC2A 4NE

British Library Cataloguing in Publication Information Available

Library of Congress Cataloging-in-Publication Data

Names: Barrett, Katherine, 1954- author. | Greene, Richard, 1955- author.
  | Kettl, Donald F., author.
Title: The little guide to writing for impact : how to communicate
  research in a way that people will read / Katherine Barrett, Richard
  Greene, and Donald F. Kettl.
Description: Lanham, Maryland : Rowman & Littlefield Publishers, [2024]
  | Includes bibliographical references and index.
Identifiers: LCCN 2023048758 (print) | LCCN 2023048759 (ebook) |
  ISBN 9781538181263 (cloth) | ISBN 9781538181270 (paperback) |
  ISBN 9781538181287 (ebook)
Subjects: LCSH: Communication in public administration. |
  Written communication. | Policy sciences.
Classification: LCC JF1525.C59 B37 2024 (print) | LCC JF1525.
  C59 (ebook) | DDC 808.06/632–dc23/eng/20240110
LC record available at https://lccn.loc.gov/2023048758
LC ebook record available at https://lccn.loc.gov/2023048759

♾️™ The paper used in this publication meets the minimum requirements
of American National Standard for Information Sciences—Permanence of
Paper for Printed Library Materials, ANSI/NISO Z39.48-1992.

We dedicate this book to Peter Harkness, Elder Witt, and Alan Ehrenhalt, a publishing and editorial team that created a "warm bath" for us in which we were able to refine our craft. And we dedicate it as well to a collection of editors over the years who have helped us sharpen our work—and who taught us how to connect with readers in learning together.

Contents

Preface

Writers in public affairs aim for impact. All writers want their writing to matter. But in public affairs, it's part of the field's DNA. There's a special imperative to write well in examining, analyzing, and attempting to solve the biggest problems facing society. Without engaging readers, these noble goals will fail to reach those who can take the words off the page and turn them into real-world policies, initiatives, and management changes.

It's also a field where authors often try to nudge busy people, engaged researchers, and (to be sure) students. So it's not only a puzzle of how best to write clearly, interestingly, and powerfully but also of how to frame writing into digestible nuggets. To practice that skill, one instructor asked students to write two-page memos. A former US senator harrumphed in reply, telling us he wouldn't read anything that long.

That's why we decided to write this guide about writing for impact. We wanted to share the lessons we've learned from decades of writing and editing, as well as to couple them with research into writing well, in the hope that our readers—and the people who read them—could benefit.

In writing this book, we began with a terrific little book by William Strunk Jr. and E. B. White, *The Elements of Style*.[1] After Strunk, an English professor at Cornell, wrote and privately published the first 1918 version for writers at the university, the book was released publicly, morphing through several editions until Strunk's death in 1946. In the late 1950s, the famous author E. B. White praised the book in his column in the *New Yorker.* That column caught the eye of an editor at Macmillan and Company, who persuaded White to expand Strunk's text. Across all its editions, the book has sold more than ten million copies and proved to be one of the many enduring contributions of White's distinguished career until his own death in 1985.

So when we decided to write this book, there was no better foundation on which to build than Strunk and White. In fact, we talked among ourselves about our "Strunk and White for public affairs" book, and that was the pitch we made to our editor. The pages that follow are decidedly not an effort to create a new *Elements of Style*, but they owe their genesis to that inestimable source. The question is how to translate the basic message of Strunk and White—write well!—into public affairs, with an eye on the emerging challenges of the twenty-first century.

The book builds on a long collaboration that we've had over many decades—and on our belief that writing well is an essential tool to gaining impact for important ideas. We've had great fun working with each other. And we hope you are infected by our enthusiasm about writing for impact in the pages that follow.

Katherine Barrett
Richard Greene
Donald F. Kettl

NOTE

1. For more information, see Maria Popova, "A Brief History of the Elements of Style and What Makes It Great," *Themarginalian* (blog), 2012, https://www.themarginalian.org/2012/02/03/stylized-elements-of-style.

Introduction

There is a flood of research about how to improve public policy, and there is an enormous hunger among practitioners and decision-makers for insights that will help them. Far too often, however, there is little connection between the supply and the demand. Researchers complain that practitioners don't pay enough attention to what they're writing. Practitioners say that much of what they read isn't understandable.

This disconnect produces a genuine loss for society. People trained in academic writing—in universities, think tanks, foundations, not-for-profits, and other organizations—have an enormous quantity of potentially powerful information to share. But if their work doesn't find its way to the people who can champion or implement programs and policies, it may bring as little value to the world as a caterpillar that placidly eats leaves but never turns into a butterfly.

As Nobel Prize–winning physicist Sir William Bragg says, "The best research is wasted when it is extremely difficult to discover what it is all about."[1] See figure I.1.

Communication is key. Sadly, training for academic writing often leads to writing that's only accessible to people trained in academic reading. As Michael Pagano, the former dean of the College of Urban Planning and Public Affairs at the University of Illinois, told us, "Many academics have been pushed to make their work more accessible. But for that to happen, academics must communicate to a more general audience in an effective way and many of them don't know how to do that now. Learning these skills is essential."[2]

It may be essential, perhaps, but the skills Pagano talks about don't necessarily come easily, particularly when academically trained writers are often praised for complexity over comprehensibility, form over substance, and expansive details over focus.

That's why we've written this book. It's been designed so that readers can quickly digest it from cover to cover, but we think that many readers will jump between the chapters, seeking answers to questions that are currently foremost on their minds.

"It is more fun to talk with someone who doesn't use long, difficult words but rather short, easy words like 'What About Lunch?'"

-- Winnie-the-Pooh by A.A. Milne

Figure I.1. Source: Wikimedia Commons, public domain (with script text added by authors from A. A. Milne Winnie-the-Pooh text, and illustration changed to jpg); credit: A. A. Milne, *Winnie-the-Pooh*, illustrator E. H. Shepard.

The lessons in the chapters are derived not just from the cumulative 110 years we've spent laboring in the groves of public administration but also from our research specifically for this book, including interviews with academics, practitioners, and editors, to discover what they think readers will find particularly useful. We also made a diligent effort to uncover the most practical guidance offered by others who have written about similar topics. One of the lessons the book communicates is the value of concrete examples, and we've taken that counsel to heart, peppering its pages with a heavy dose of them. We've even taken the perilous step of including illustrative examples—both positive and negative—from our own work.

Of course, writing about writing has a built-in danger. In the chapters that follow, readers will find an assortment of basic rules. It's inevitable that all writers—including the three of us—break them occasionally (sometimes with intent, sometimes not).

So give us a break if you see that we've occasionally overused a word, started sentences with vague references, ended with a preposition, or used too many adjectives. Nobody's perfect.

WHO CAN BENEFIT FROM THIS BOOK?

This book, we believe, will prove of interest to a wide range of writers:

- University-based academics whose work intersects with public administration and policy and who need to communicate the results of their research clearly
- Researchers at academically oriented think tanks and foundations
- Academics at universities who want to find an audience for their work beyond the world of other universities
- Researchers writing for the all-important journals that elevate their standing in the community

- Students—both at graduate and undergraduate levels—who are preparing for careers in research and public service, as well as those enrolled in public policy courses
- Academically trained authors of policy briefs and other documents, including legislative staffers and anyone intent on communicating with policy makers
- Mid-career professionals who want to advance their careers by getting public attention for their pragmatic insights

WHEN YOU'RE FINISHED WITH THIS BOOK, WHAT WILL YOU KNOW?

When you get to the end, what will you have learned? For one thing, you'll know some things you already knew before you began reading. Reinforcement of good habits is invaluable.

We predict, however, that the information you'll find here will help you to commit resolutely to good habits you've already developed as well as to consider and apply a variety of other skills that you haven't absorbed in the past.

Among other things, we seek to provide you with the ability to keep your writing simple and clear, write to the needs of your audience, write to the length desired by editors and readers, keep your writing interesting, avoid techniques that may be fine for a dissertation but not for other writing tasks, use graphics and other visual techniques to communicate, get the facts right, pitch your ideas in order to get them published, enlist friends and colleagues to advance your cause, work well with editors, use social media, and so on.

A couple of the messages that trickle through this book are the benefits of brevity and getting right to the point. So we'll practice what we preach and end this introduction here.

Read on and enjoy.

NOTES

1. Quoted by Thomas Rice Henn, *The Apple and the Spectroscope: Being Lectures on Poetry Designed (in the Main) for Science Students* (Abingdon, UK: Routledge, 1951), 142.

2. Interview with authors, April 5, 2023.

Chapter 1

Write for Aunt Tillie

Simple, Clear Writing Is King

You surely get lots of questions about the project you're working on. What do you tell people? And how can you prevent the my-eyes-glaze-over (MEGO) syndrome when you tell your relatives about the new, exciting issue you're researching?

Researchers working on important but often technical topics find that questions about their work can be difficult to answer, even when their audience is in the same room. It's even harder when information is communicated in written form. One of the authors, in fact, once was on the operating table, and the anesthesiologist asked about a book in progress. The author started to explain all the pieces that seemed fascinating—and the anesthesiologist quickly reached for the mask and turned on the gas. The author nodded off, and the anesthesiologist was spared having to administer the gas to himself.

The key to cracking this problem is to write for your Aunt Tillie. Everyone has an Aunt Tillie: a nonexpert/nongeek nonresearcher who is the prototype of a general reader. Let's describe her a bit: Aunt Tillie doesn't know much about the topic; she's easily distracted; she wants to know how your topic applies to her; she has a very limited attention span; but, as your aunt, she's willing to be persuaded.

If you can capture Aunt Tillie's imagination, you'll appeal to a broad collection of people who can benefit from your work as well.

WILL ANYONE READ WHAT YOU WRITE?

There is some interesting research—and a lot of urban legends—about how many published pieces actually are read. One 2007 journal article, for example, concluded that as many as 50 percent of papers are never read by anyone except editors and referees.[1]

Gulp.

Those numbers have worried authors for years.

Fortunately, there are ways to increase the odds that readers will read the words you write. We'll try to give you some approaches in the paragraphs that follow. It's all pretty simple: if you write for Aunt Tillie in clear language, you will open the front door of your article, blog post, commentary, paper, or book—and crack it open much more widely for readers who aren't sure whether they really want to enter.

Of course, many authors in technical fields, including public affairs, reject the idea that ordinary readers ought to be able to connect with what they write. They write for professionals, they say. In our experience, however, writing for Aunt Tillie helps you connect far better with these readers too. It helps you reach people who find your topic fascinating but who might not have ordinarily picked up your work.

LEAVING THE FRONT DOOR OPEN

There are a few basic approaches to help readers want to read what you have to say:

Choose a good title. This can be the first introduction to readers about your work and what it's about. If the title is long or confusing, impatient readers may move elsewhere rapidly and never have a chance to learn from what you've written. Many people who are trained in academic writing are inclined to write titles that go on and on until they've basically written the first line of the piece.

Frame your thesis early on. Any informative writing ought to have a thesis. Having that clearly in your mind and then presenting it in a straightforward way will lure your readers in. We're fond of telling doctoral students that their thesis ought to have a thesis. Some journalists call this a "nut graph," which Wylie Communications defines like this: "The nut graph—aka the 'billboard' or the 'so-what graph'—is where you put the story into a nutshell. It explains why the story is timely and provides the kernel, or central theme, of your piece."[2]

Craft a great abstract for your paper. As we describe later in chapter 8, in academic writing, the abstract is your chance to make a pitch to readers about what you are trying to say and why it matters. Many readers will never go past the first paragraph if you don't clarify why they should—in plain English. What is the basic question you're trying to answer? What theoretical puzzles does your paper connect to? How are you exploring them? What findings do you have? And most fundamentally, what's the story you're trying to tell? Think about telling this to Aunt Tillie when you're crafting your tale.

Go out with a bang. There's one more thing. Once you've intrigued your readers thoroughly enough to get them to keep reading, be sure to write a great conclusion. A short excursion into "questions for future research" can work, but you don't want the paper to end by appearing to push big questions off to another researcher or to your own future project. That can only undermine the work at hand. What have you accomplished in *this* paper?

What's more, simply ending a piece with the last fact you want to share will leave readers up in the air. This is the rhetorical equivalent of the "need for closure," a phrase coined by social psychologist Arie Kruglanski in the 1990s.[3] There's a parallel between this psychological term and the conclusion to your work.

As the Association for Psychological Science puts it, closure is a framework "for decision making that aims to find an answer on a given topic that will alleviate confusion or ambiguity."[4]

That's what your last paragraph or two should do. (For more about conclusions, see chapter 12.)

KISS

In a couple of chapters, we're going to rail on a bit about the need to avoid acronyms when they may not be easily understood. But we've consciously broken this rule with the subhead for this section. KISS is shorthand for "Keep it simple, stupid," which keeps readers going after you've gotten them to start (see figure 1.1).

Avoiding jargon is key. Careful technical language helps to avoid confusion, of course. Air traffic controllers for the Federal Aviation Administration, for example, have developed very precise terms for guiding aircraft both in the sky and on the ground to prevent collisions, as several crashes in the past occurred when

Figure 1.1. KISS. Source: From Getty Images, Creative #149297027; credit: Getty Images/Raywoo.

controllers thought they were saying one thing and pilots heard something different. A poor reason for using technical language is to make it sound like you know what you're talking about. That obstructs easy reading and drives readers away.

Fluid, powerful sentences and paragraphs are the building blocks of good writing. But consider the lesson learned by every child who has ever played with blocks: You need to think through the order in which you place them, and not just select the ones closest to you. That would only cause your tower to come crashing to the floor.

So though it can be tempting to write in the order in which ideas occur to you, that's likely not the order a reader can find most helpful. The World Bank's guide to report writing offers some counsel and a variety of alternatives: "In addition to having good topic sentences, paragraphs must have a clear and logical organization. There are many ways to organize paragraphs."[5]

Among the most obvious ways to structure something is through chronology. First, this happened, then that happened, and here's how things are now. That is certainly simple, but it can easily lead to spending far too much space writing about less interesting history without focusing on the big picture now—or why the history is important.

Another approach—one that will seem familiar from a great deal that you read—is the "inverted pyramid." This writing technique has been in common use for more than a century, and it organizes information in descending order of importance. As Jasmine Roberts writes in Ohio State University's *Writing for Strategic Communication Industries*, "This allows the audience to read the most crucial details quickly so they can decide whether to continue or stop reading the story."[6]

Here's another idea. You start with your thesis, expand on that, then provide the countervailing evidence, and wind up by synthesizing the two. This thesis-antithesis-synthesis triad is often misattributed to German philosopher Georg Wilhelm Friedrich Hegel, but the origins of the idea aren't crucial. It can work for you.

There are obviously multiple other structures you can use. But if the paragraphs build on each other and the first sentence of every paragraph gives readers an idea of how the paper is building, you'll be okay. One trick here: See if you can skim through what you've written as quickly as you can, with a focus on the first sentence of the paragraphs. If you emerge with a general idea of what the piece was about, that's a good sign.

AVOID OFFENSE

There's no place for gender-limiting language in writing. For a very long time, "he" was the pronoun of choice for writers, and that left out half of the human race. Writers tried to correct that by using "he or she," but that often turned out to be awkward. "They" has begun to emerge, but not everyone has yet accepted it. An easy solution is to pluralize. Instead of writing that "He couldn't defend himself" when referring to a person who could be male, female, or nonbinary, try the plural: "Public figures have a hard time defending themselves when they've been the target of media attacks." That is smoother and avoids the awkward use of "they" in the singular.

More generally, be careful about your word choice. The *New York Times* developed a quiz on words that readers might not want to depend on anymore.[7] (Note the plural used here to avoid falling into the gender trap.) Words about race, for example, have an uncomfortable place in the public dialogue. Terms including "Latinx" and "Asian American Pacific Islander" have not yet fully caught on, in part because of established usage and in part because there continues to be a debate about whether to include Fiji islanders and residents from China in the same group. Many Black Americans prefer "Black," but some editors continue to debate whether it should be capitalized—and, if so, whether that means "White" ought to be capitalized as well. The AP Stylebook editors have determined that while the *B* in Black is upper case, the *w* in white isn't.

It can be quite confusing, but one thing is clear: as language and its usage evolve, writers need to be thoughtful about the words they choose and not assume that yesterday's acceptable verbiage will be acceptable today.

TALK TO YOUR DOG

All of these tips will help you communicate with Aunt Tillie—and colleagues in your field. The most important point of all, though, is formulating an idea that is sharp and clear. The early 140-character limit on Twitter had one great virtue: if you can capture the point of your paper in 140 characters, you can explain it to everyone.

How do you do that? One of us talks to the dog, who never argues back and who often proves an exceptionally good audience (see figure 1.2). Long walks have a good way of focusing the mind, and it is always rewarding to get a happy response (at least as long as there are treats involved). In fact, the dog is in the

Figure 1.2. Source: From Getty Images, Creative #1149830948; credit: Getty Images/Jozef Polc/500px.

lap of one of the authors while drafting this paragraph, and talking it over with her has given the author a chance to hear what the idea sounds like before committing it to paper. Other people find talking to roommates or a conversation with a good friend over a favorite beverage helpful.

The core of the idea is this. Especially with a good computer, it's easy to pour words out onto a page. To ensure that those words have a beating heart, though, it's often useful to talk out loud about what you are working on and why it matters. Sometimes even the most difficult ideas snap into sharp focus when the writer hears how the words sound out loud. More than one dissertation student has benefited by escaping the library and answering the adviser's fundamental question: What are you trying to say here?

And that can give you the warm-up you need for telling Aunt Tillie what you're working on.

FROM OUR KEYBOARDS

From Don Kettl in *Governing*, October 2022: "With Hurricane Ian barreling down on Florida in late September, Mark and Rhonda Wilkerson decided to hunker down and ride out the storm. But unlike thousands of other residents of the Fort Myers area, their home didn't even lose a shingle."[8]

Does this make you want to keep reading to learn *how* the Wilkersons escaped the disaster that Ian inflicted on so many other families?

NOTES

1. Lokman I. Meho, "The Rise and Rise of Citation Analysis," *Physics World* 20, no. 1 (2007): 32, https://iopscience.iop.org/article/10.1088/2058-7058/20/1/33.

2. Ann Wylie, "How to Write a Nut Graf, or Nut Graph," *Wylie Communications* (blog), https://www.wyliecomm.com/2019/10/how-to-write-a-nut-graf (accessed November 2, 2023).

3. "The Psychology of Closure and Why Some Need It More than Others," Association for Psychological Science, published October 16, 2018, https://www.psychologicalscience.org/news/the-psychology-of-closure-and-why-some-need-it-more-than-others.html.

4. "The Psychology of Closure," Association for Psychological Science.

5. "Organizing Paragraphs," Report Writing at The World Bank, Cole-learning.net, published 2012, http://colelearning.net/rw_wb/module5/page10.html.

6. Jasmine Roberts, *Writing for Strategic Communication Industries* (Columbus: The Ohio State University, 2016), 48, https://ohiostate.pressbooks.pub/stratcommwriting.

7. Quoctrung Bui, Sara Chodosh, Jessica Bennett, and John McWhorter, "Quiz: You Can't Say That (Or Can You?)," *New York Times*, December 22, 2022, https://www.nytimes.com/interactive/2022/12/22/opinion/words-you-cant-use-anymore.html.

8. Donald F. Kettl, "The Storms That Test Local Governments," *Governing*, October 26, 2022, https://www.governing.com/community/the-storms-that-test-local-governments.

Chapter 2

One Size Doesn't Fit All

Make Sure You Know Your Audience

Not long ago, one of us was sitting in on an editorial board meeting of the *Washington Post*. Inevitably, the book and film about the Watergate Affair, *All the President's Men*, came to mind. They provided an inside view of the battles between editors over the limited space on the front page.

But this editorial board meeting wasn't much like the historic images. The question on the table was about which items on the paper's website at the moment were drawing the most readers—and how soon they ought to be rotated off the website to make room for new stories that might produce even more. The editors took half the meeting to work through the internet options before turning to the classic discussion of the next day's front page.

Writers need to think like those editors. The *Post* team sought to know their audience as well as possible. Some writers focus mainly on what sounds good to them, but that risks a disconnect with readers—and a great idea that slinks off to the corner to die.

DIFFERENT PUBLICATIONS HAVE
DIFFERENT AUDIENCES

Editors—or at least the successful ones—usually have a keen eye for knowing what their readers will want to read. Consider how several news sources covered the April 2023 arrest of Jack Teixeira, the twenty-one-year-old member of the Massachusetts Air National Guard who was alleged to have posted national security secrets on Discord, a major messaging site.

The *New York Times* headlined its online story. "Airman Faces Two Counts Related to Leaked Documents."[1] Here's the first paragraph: "Jack Teixeira, a 21-year-old member of the Massachusetts Air National Guard, was charged with two counts related to retaining and distributing classified and national defense information."[2]

The *New York Post*, on the other hand, often goes for more attention-grabbing angles. Its headline was "Pentagon Leak Suspect Jack Teixeira Hit with Two Federal Charges," and it went for a more personal beginning, which emphasized Teixeira's relationship with his father: "The Air National Guardsman accused of leaking a trove of classified US documents was hauled to court Friday on federal charges—telling his dad he loved him during the brief hearing."[3]

Then *Fox News* had the following headline: "Arrest of Classified Documents Leak Suspect Jack Teixeira Met with Outrage: 'Incompetence Is Stunning.'"[4] And here's how *Fox News* started: "The arrest of a 21-year-old Air National Guardsman in connection to classified documents that have been leaked online in recent months has been met with outrage as critics wonder how a young man could have such high-level access to national security information."[5]

That news outlet focused on the ongoing leak as a transparent criticism of the Biden administration because Fox's audience has eaten up that kind of outlook.

All these news sources work hard to maximize the number of readers. They do that by working hard to understand their audience.

TACTICS AND STRATEGIES

When writers try to convert their words into actionable information, some approaches prove especially useful.

Pick your audience first. Before trying to write something or pitching it to the appropriate editor, consider the audience you're most likely to reach. To reach an audience of practitioners for something about public sector budgeting, for example, you'd want to think about the recently launched *Public Finance Journal,* the brainchild of the Government Finance Officers Association. But if you want to write about a similar topic—but for an academic audience with an international slant—then you might think of the *International Journal of Public Administration.*

Read, read, and read again. It's startling how many writers decide they've found an appropriate outlet for their work, but they know very little about it. If there's a good editor in charge, the contents of any publication will reveal the nature of the audience. That, in turn, should guide your writing.

Think about demographics. In writing this book, we're hoping to attract readers who cross a wide swath of age ranges, including people still trying to get advanced degrees. As a result, even though the authors of this book might want to allude to movies like *Casablanca* or *Citizen Kane*, we've tried to make sure to refer to *Guardians of the Galaxy* as well. A similar rule applies here. If the audience for a publication is made up entirely of academics, then you can be a little more technically complex in your writing than if the audience is largely made up of practitioners. For a piece aimed at a younger audience, metaphors and similes should fit into their scope of knowledge. When teaching, we often ask ourselves, "What's the first political memory of the students in front

Figure 2.1. Source: From Getty Images, Creative #97212213; credit: Getty Images/CSA Images.

of us?" That provides a keen insight into the issues and examples that would best connect with the class.

Take the time to study which articles in the publication had the most citations. It stands to reason that one measure of audience interest is citations, and publications will be most eager to publish articles that are likely to get many. There is one cautionary note here: there are lots of issues that sit behind these numbers, including the window of time used for collecting the data and what counts as a citation. There are lots of games for boosting a citation count.[6] And individual disciplines often have different citation conventions, so the numbers can vary a great deal and are hard to take fully at face value. Even so, many people pay attention to them, especially when it comes to making promotion decisions in universities.

Know that academic presses are very different from trade presses. Among book publishers, there's an enormous gulf between academic presses, which seek to break even but specialize in featuring interesting books that will advance theory, and trade presses, which seek a far broader audience and larger profits. Trade press editors are always looking for the next bestseller. Academic presses love bestsellers too—Princeton University Press hit no. 1 on the *New York Times Best Seller* list with Harry G. Frankfurt's *On Bullshit*—but they typically don't insist on as high a level of projected sales before signing the contract for a book.

Consider even the subtlest differences between publications. Lumping all academic publications into one huge pile is as big a mistake as thinking that the audience for National Public Radio is the same as that for Fox News. For example, both *Public Administration Review* and *Journal of Public Administration Research and Theory* publish articles about public administration and public management. *Public Administration Review* seeks an audience of both academics and practitioners, and its articles tend to take a somewhat more conversational approach, as shown by the headline and abstract opening of this 2020 paper:

Headline: Municipal Structure Matters: Evidence from Government Fiscal Performance

Abstract first sentence: Evidence for the fundamental presumption that municipal structure matters for government performance is smaller and weaker than many might expect.[7]

This article, by contrast, ran in the *Journal of Public Administration Research and Theory:*

Headline: Management, Organizational Performance, and Task Clarity: Evidence from Ghana's Civil Service

Abstract first sentence: We study the relationship between management practices, organizational performance, and task clarity, using observational data analysis on an original survey of the universe of Ghanaian civil servants across 45 organizations and novel administrative data on over 3,600 tasks they undertake.[8]

Understand the big differences between the audiences for books and articles. Some authors attempt to bundle papers that were previously published in academic journals as a book for submission to a book editor. This is a mistake. A book needs to flow from the introduction through its conclusion, with a series of chapters that develop an intriguing argument that carefully links the chapters. Chapters lifted from previous journal articles typically do not have that connection. Moreover, most book editors are reluctant to publish books that have substantial pieces that have appeared in print elsewhere.

A book needs a narrative spine, with the chapters built logically. Individual papers bundled together typically do not do that.

If you want to publish your ideas in a book, carefully research possible presses. One good way to start is to stack up your favorite books in your field and check who published them. Another way is to discover presses that might be open to your ideas based on what appears on their website. No academic press publishes books about everything. Each one develops what the presses call a list, which is often organized in different series—for example, a series on political philosophy and another on education policy. Mentors can help you find the best audience for your project.

Understand that no matter how great an idea you have for a book, there will always be a sales projection that goes behind every editor's analysis. Academic presses will typically be a better opportunity for younger authors than trade presses.

FROM OUR KEYBOARDS

From Barrett and Greene: Two articles about a very similar topic were published within weeks of one another. The topic was data quality.

Here's the first paragraph of a column we wrote for the general-interest website Route Fifty, which has an audience almost entirely made up of readers in the United States:

> There's nothing new about the importance of data to the smooth functioning of state and local government. But over the last few years, with the aid of advancing technology, phrases like "data-driven" have become ubiquitous and are used to make it appear that policies that fit in that category have some kind of magical seal of reliability.[9]

But the *International Journal for Public Administration* has an audience that spreads around the world, so we packaged similar findings into a commentary that began like this:

> With advances in technology, governments across the world are increasingly using data to help inform their decision making. This has been one of the most important by-products of the use of open data, which is "a philosophy—and increasingly a set of policies—that promotes transparency, accountability and value creation by making government data available to all," according to the Organisation for Economic Co-operation.[10]

NOTES

1. "Airman Faces Two Counts Related to Leaked Documents," *New York Times*, April 14, 2023, https://www.nytimes.com/live/2023/04/14/us/leaked-documents-jack-teixeira.

2. "Airman Faces Two Counts," *New York Times*.

3. Andy Tillett and Olivia Land, "Pentagon Leak Suspect Jack Teixeira Hit with Two Federal Charges," *New York Post*, April 14, 2023, https://nypost.com/2023/04/14/pentagon-leak-suspect-jack-teixeira-hit-with-two-federal-charges.

4. Maria Lencki, "Arrest of Classified Documents Leak Suspect Jack Teixeira Met with Outrage: 'Incompetence Is Stunning,'" Fox News, April 13, 2023, https://www.foxnews.com/media/arrest-classified-documents-leak-suspect-jack-teixeira-met-outrage-incompetence-stunning.

5. Lencki, "Arrest of Classified Documents," Fox News.

6. Phil Davis, "Gaming Google Scholar Citations, Made Simple and Easy," *The Scholarly Kitchen* (blog), December 12, 2012, https://scholarlykitchen.sspnet.org/2012/12/12/gaming-google-scholar-citations-made-simple-and-easy.

7. Wenchi Wei, "Municipal Structure Matters: Evidence from Government Fiscal Performance," *Public Administration Review* 82, no. 1 (2020): 160–73, https://onlinelibrary.wiley.com/doi/epdf/10.1111/puar.13183.

8. Imran Rasul, Daniel Rogger, Martin J. Williams, "Management, Organizational Performance, and Task Clarity: Evidence from Ghana's Civil Service," *Journal of Public Administration Research and Theory* 31, no. 2 (April 2021): 259–77, https://academic.oup.com/jpart/article/31/2/259/5974047?searchresult=1.

9. Katherine Barrett and Richard Greene, "Data-Based Decision Making Is Flawed When the Data Is Flawed," Route Fifty, March 2, 2023, https://www.route-fifty.com/digital-government/2023/03/data-based-decision-making-flawed-when-data-flawed/383539.

10. Katherine Barrett and Richard Greene, "As the Quantity of Data Explodes, Quality Matters," *International Journal of Public Administration* 0, issue ahead-of-print (March 31, 2023), https://www.tandfonline.com/doi/full/10.1080/01900692.2023.2197171.

Chapter 3

Escaping Inside Baseball

Shortcuts Can Drive
Your Readers Away

When writing for people in your own discipline, it's easy to get away with using jargon that insiders understand. Experts sometimes refer to this as "inside baseball," which is from the idea that baseball pros and fans often use a jumble of phrases to describe a play in terms only understood by pros and other fans; for example: "The home team picked up a couple of runs in the bottom of the fifth through a combination of bunting, stealing, using the hit-and-run, and cleverly executing a squeeze play. But the visiting team countered with skillful management of its bullpen for the rest of the game, especially with the closer."

As the late wordsmith extraordinaire William Safire defines "inside baseball" in a *New York Times Magazine* column in 1988, "From its sports context comes its political or professional denotation: minutiae savored by the cognoscenti, delicious details, nuances discussed and dissected by aficionados."[1]

Safire is clearly having fun at writers' expense. One of the basic concepts of writing for impact is reaching outside the inner circle of experts and clearly expressing thoughts in a way that will be comprehensible—and even enjoyable—to a far larger audience, including policymakers, practitioners, and even the general public. Key to this is avoiding four traps: jargon, acronyms, complex numeric explanations, and the use of excessive footnoting as an excuse to avoid needed explanations.

JARGON

"Jargon masks real meaning," Jennifer Chatman, management professor in the Haas School of Business at the University of California, Berkeley, is quoted as saying in a *Forbes* article.[2] "People use it as a substitute for thinking hard and clearly about their goals and the direction that they want to give others."[3]

An article titled "Keeping the Jargon Out of Public Communication," published by a network of government officials called GovLoop, notes that phrases such as "entrepreneurial management paradigm" roll off the tongue of public administrators who write for professional journals more readily than explaining that there is a belief that private-sector techniques would improve public management.[4]

Some years ago, a couple of the authors of this book were called upon to consult with the Governmental Accounting Standards Board, the independent organization that establishes accounting and financial reporting standards for US state and local governments. The goal was to explore the idea of encouraging staff to write in plain English.

After a laborious exercise that involved revising one of its documents so that the average nonaccountant could understand it, a meeting was held with the staff and the board itself. Board members seemed moderately eager to go down this road, but the staff stridently resisted. They contended that, in the world of government reporting, precision is key. Using words that could have multiple meanings risked producing financial reports that could be understood differently by different people. Jargon, they said, was important, though they didn't use the word "jargon."

In this case, the board determined that it was more important to reach document users than to attract a broader audience. But for readers of this book who are concerned with reaching someone outside of their immediate circle of experts, technical jargon just gets in the way.

One impediment to draining the jargon out of your prose can be identifying what is genuinely jargon. It's easy to assume that any words familiar to you are also familiar to others. One way around this is to ask someone who lacks expertise in a topic to read through a piece of writing and identify the words that aren't abundantly clear.

A handful of phrases that easily sneak their way into text—and which a good editor will seek out and replace—include value proposition, logic model, intentionality, control variables, and big data. That last was a hot buzzword in the mid-2010s, but a series of interviews with people in the public sector revealed that these two seemingly simple words had different meanings depending on who was using them. The only general agreement was that "big data" was desirable, but it wasn't clear whether it was the data, the dataset, or the ideas that were "big." In fact, it was never clear how "big" data needed to be before qualifying as "big."

ACRONYMS

There are certain acronyms that are generally understood and don't need to be spelled out. Nobody really needs to use the Federal Bureau of Investigation instead of FBI. Similarly, CIA is a perfectly reasonable acronym for the Central Intelligence Agency.

There are even some acronyms that have entirely replaced the words they originally stood for. Who among us can easily identify the origins of radar as "radio detection and ranging" or scuba as "self-contained underwater breathing apparatus"? Then there's the generally accepted, uncontroversial acronym snafu, which originally was an acronym for "situation normal, all fouled up." (Though the word "fouled" was often replaced by another word beginning with the letter f.)

The acronyms that just confuse matters, however, far outnumber those that have fallen into general usage. One example is ESG, which stands for environmental, social, and business governance and can be used as a device to screen for investments in companies that tend to be socially conscious. This acronym fell into disrepute in several states where leaders viewed it as a kind of governmental overreach. We won't go into the politics here, but we'll bet the royalties on one copy of this book that many of the opponents of ESG don't have the foggiest notion of what those three letters stand for.

That may be an extreme case because of the political overtone, but one thing is clear: when acronyms distract from true understanding—that is, when acronyms create a speed bump for readers—they should be avoided. (See figure 3.1.)

Consider this paragraph from a report by an organization typically called PEER, which stands for Mississippi's Joint Legislative Committee on Performance Evaluation and Expenditure Review. (In keeping with the theme of this chapter, a minority of people familiar with the organization would be likely to know the full name.) It's loaded with acronyms that make reading difficult, even though they are all spelled out elsewhere in the same document:

Unlike some agencies granted exemption from MSPB oversight (e.g., the Mississippi Department of Education in FYs 2015 and

Figure 3.1. Source: Created by authors from free word cloud creation website.

2016), MDCPS was not exempt from MSPB's regulations regarding staff compensation; therefore, MDCPS was required to adjust salaries in accordance with MSPB's VCP.[5]

Huh?

Want a little more evidence that acronyms should be avoided? The following eight can be found in a variety of documents. Take a look and see how many you can immediately identify. They are spelled out at the end of this chapter, and we guess that any of you who get seven or more have done much better than the average reader.

- BAFO
- RFI
- VOSB
- STEM
- SLG
- CISO
- HEDIS
- FOIA

NUMERIC EXPLANATIONS

Sometimes it can be important to explain the math behind a conclusion that you're reaching. The numbers matter in proving a point.

But when prose grows gritty with numbers, it can easily become impenetrable. So the key is to simplify when possible. Consider the use of percentages. A paragraph may be justifiably full of them in order to put a situation in perspective. But overuse can tend to impede easy reading.

Rather than writing that 63 percent of residents of Numbertown, USA, are enjoying the parks, it might be better to try something like this: "Out of every 100 residents of Numbertown, 63 of them enjoy the parks." That phrasing humanizes the issue.

Many academic publications rely on formulas to prove a thesis, and for quantitative work, that can be necessary. But when it's time to turn a dissertation into an article, wise communicators excise formulas and opt for text to explain what they mean. If writers can't do that, it may be a sign that they don't really understand the inner workings of the formula or even what it means. And that's a bad sign.

FOOTNOTING

Writing for academic journals requires references, whether as footnotes or endnotes. It's vitally important that academic readers can follow the sources of your arguments. But when it's time to translate a purely academic piece of prose into one for more general use, you'll find that much of the time, footnotes or endnotes aren't permissible when writing something other than a book (this one, for example, is chock full of them).

One solution for online writing is to use hyperlinks. These marvels of modern technology allow readers to quickly flash to the source document to enhance their reading experience. But beware of overusing hyperlinks too. There's always a risk that when a reader jumps to an article you provide as a source, they'll get so interested in that piece of writing that they'll run out of time before coming back to yours. Moreover, a blizzard of links can distract readers from the flow of an argument.

What's more, online addresses can frequently change, so just a few months after you've published something, it's nearly inevitable that at least one of the hyperlinks may no longer lead anyplace except to the frustrating "404 error" message.

Even when writing for an academic audience, a surfeit of footnotes, endnotes, citations, and quotes may chase away your audience. Readers will want to know the sources on which you're relying—and that you're relying on sources rather than going off on your personal tangent. But it's always worth asking whether the quotations and citations you use are moving your argument forward.

Littering your text with an overabundance of external references is usually a mistake. Writers sometimes think that the quality of their research can be measured by the number of citations. Rather than draw your readers in, an excessive number of notes may invite readers to skip past a section of your paper, assuming that they have seen all this literature elsewhere—or that the reliance on notes means that you don't have original ideas of your own to contribute. What they really want to know is why they ought to read *your* paper, what original contributions you will be making, and how it builds on previous work in the field.

The Acronym Quiz Answers

BAFO—In procurement, best and final offer

RFI—Request for information

VOSB—Veteran owned small business

STEM—Science, technology, engineering, and math in an educational program

SLG—State and local government

CISO—Chief information security officer

HEDIS—Healthcare Effectiveness Data and Information Set

FOIA—Freedom of Information Act

NOTES

1. William Safire, "On Language; Inside Baseball," *New York Times Magazine*, June 19, 1988, https://www.nytimes.com/1988/06/19/magazine/on-language-inside-baseball.html.

2. Max Mallet, Brett Nelson, and Chris Steiner, "The Most Annoying, Pretentious and Useless Business Jargon," *Forbes*, January 26, 2012, https://www.forbes.com/sites/groupthink/2012/01/26/the-most-annoying-pretentious-and-useless-business-jargon/?sh=64f4ad8a2eea.

3. Mallet, Nelson, and Steiner, "The Most Annoying, Pretentious."

4. "Keeping the Jargon Out of Public Communication," GovLoop, published June 12, 2012, https://www.govloop.com/community/blog/keeping-the-jargon-out-of-public-communication/.

5. Joint Legislative Committee on Performance Evaluation and Expenditure Review, State of Mississippi, *A Review of the Exemption of the Mississippi Department of Child Protective Services from Mississippi State Personnel Board Oversight,* Issue Brief 670 (June 14, 2022), https://da.mdah.ms.gov/series/legislature/peer-su/detail/923778 (accessed November 2, 2023).

Chapter 4

Good Writing Is Like Good Music

Keep Your Writing Interesting So Readers Will Stay for the Finale

George Gershwin's music (as seen in figure 4.1) may not sound much like Rihanna's. But they share one trait. People who enjoy their melodies stay tuned from the beginning of a song until the end. The same is true for well-wrought prose.

It may seem that elaborate writing, full of multisyllabic words and fancy flourishes, will convince the reader that you have something important to say. But that's not true. If a writer provides

Figure 4.1.   Gershwin Sheet Music. Source: WikimediaCommons: Rhap in blue opening.jpg; credit: Wikimedia Commons/Tjako van Schie.

concrete evidence of the points being made, there's no need to hide behind complicated verbiage.

As author Eric Larson has written about Winston Churchill, he "attacked the cumbersome prose that so often marked official reports."[1] Larson quotes Churchill as saying that well-written documents "may at first seem rough as compared with the flat surface of officialese jargon. But the saving of time will be great, while the discipline of setting out the real points concisely will prove an aid to clear thinking."[2]

There are no magic tricks that ensure that readers will stay tuned from the first sentence to the last, but there are several devices that can help. This chapter offers a series of specific ideas that you should bear in mind when you sit down at your keyboard, yellow legal pad, or microphone.

GRAB YOUR READERS IN THE FIRST PARAGRAPHS

In journalistic circles the first paragraphs of a column or an article are called the lede (pronounced "leed"). That may seem like a funny spelling, but it's been used in newsrooms since at least the 1950s to avoid confusion between the lead paragraph in an article and the metal lead (pronounced "led"), which was used to set type in the days before computers.

One key to kicking off a piece is to avoid "throat-clearing" sentences. Say, for example, you're writing about a study that explores the melting of Antarctic ice because of climate change. There may be a temptation to begin with words like this: "Climate change is one of the most serious threats to the world today, along with war, famine, and disease. For some time, it was easy to ignore this issue, but ever since Al Gore came out with his film, *An Inconvenient Truth*, more and more Americans have been awakened to the potential of this imminent crisis, which could easily disrupt life in America and the rest of the planet."

All are pretty enough words, but there is nothing that gets to the point or engages readers who have already read dozens of articles about the broad topic of climate change.

Much better was the lede to this Reuters article that read, "Rapidly melting Antarctic ice is dramatically slowing down the flow of water through the world's oceans, and could have a disastrous impact on global climate, the marine food chain and even the stability of ice shelves."[3] That does a good job of giving the reader an idea of what's to follow and making it seem like there's intriguing information to come.

The most important part of the lede, naturally enough, is the very first sentence. Consider this example from fiction. Leo Tolstoy's *Anna Karenina* begins as follows: "All happy families are alike; each unhappy family is unhappy in its own way."[4] Who could lose interest after a first line like that?

One other piece of counsel that works for many (if not all) writers as they structure their first paragraphs is from a blog post about songwriting featured by NineBuzz Music Apps. It seems particularly apt, given the title of this chapter. The blog post provides the following advice:

Start with the End in Mind.

I think this tip applies to all writing and storytelling vehicles. For example, when I started writing this blog post, I outlined it. I knew how it was going to end. This really helps facilitate writing and I believe leads to a better quality more deliberative product.[5]

USE PARAGRAPHS THE WAY THEY WERE INTENDED

As Matt Ellis writes in a blog post in Grammarly, a grammar-checking and writing app:

Simply put, a paragraph is a collection of sentences all related to a central topic, idea, or theme. Paragraphs act as structural tools for writers to organize their thoughts into an ideal progression, and they also help readers process those thoughts effortlessly. Imagine how much harder reading and writing would be if everything was just one long block of text.[6]

That's simple enough. And yet many paragraphs written in academese do just the opposite. For example, we came across a paper that was written for a journal about science and public policy. One single paragraph in the report ran a full 210 words. To put that into perspective, that's nearly four times the length of the first paragraph of the Matt Ellis blog post we quote at the beginning of this section.

The Writing Center at the University of North Carolina offers some concrete advice about paragraphs. Excerpts include the following advice, saying that paragraphs should be:

Unified: "All of the sentences in a single paragraph should be related to a single controlling idea."

Clearly related to the thesis: "The sentences should all refer to the central idea, or thesis, of the paper."

Coherent: "The sentences should be arranged in a logical manner and should follow a definite plan for development."

Well-developed: "Every idea discussed in the paragraph should be adequately explained and supported through evidence and details."

Of varying length: "Many students define paragraphs in terms of length. . . . In reality, though, the unity and coherence of ideas among sentences is what constitutes a paragraph."[7]

One powerful device for making pungent prose is to vary the length of both sentences and paragraphs. When either ramble on, readers can get lost on their way to the point. Sometimes a short, one-sentence paragraph can be particularly powerful. There are those who contend that good academic writing cannot have a one-sentence paragraph.[8]

Those people are wrong.

Of course, in journalistic writing, different attitudes and styles prevail. Short paragraphs are far more common, as they ease reading and are used to emphasize key points or significant quotes. This approach can also be useful in reaching public figures whose limited time only allows a quick skim of a proposal or research finding that could potentially influence decision making.

MAKE THE MOST OUT OF METAPHORS AND SIMILES

Metaphors and similes can make writing come to life, and they're best when original (or else they fall into the category of clichés to be avoided). You don't need to be Shakespeare to come up with enticing metaphors ("But soft, what light through yonder window breaks? It is the east, and Juliet is the sun!"[9]). As Jason Collins writes in in a blog post for *Impactio*:

> Because we're taught early that academic and conversational language should be two totally different levels of speech, it's often considered a no-no to sprinkle metaphors and analogies in research writing. But it's actually possible, and often impressive, to use an appropriate figure of speech in your technical text, as long as it flows naturally and helps promote an understanding of a concept in a way that scientific jargon might not otherwise allow.[10]

Even those of us whose prose won't be around in hundreds of years can use these potent devices.

TAKE ADVANTAGE OF THE POWER OF THE VERB

There's a real temptation to liven up your prose with artistic adjectives and adverbs, but it's the verbs that really make prose sing. It may be that the word "walked" is the first one that comes to mind in writing a sentence, but consider how much more of an evocative, precise image emerges with verbs that better describe how the person is walking. Perhaps they're strolling, sauntering, or even lurching. One English teacher offers a cogent example in EdPlace, the website for homeschooling:

> Think of all the different words we have for "said"—whispered, groaned, screamed, cried, laughed, mumbled, explained . . . there are a plethora of examples. If you switch out "said" and replace it with a more powerful verb instead, your writing instantly transforms, evolving into something more descriptive and varied. This helps your reader interpret how . . . your character . . . feels; for example, you can change a general conversation into a shouting match.[11]

Here is one cautionary note about using "said" options when quoting someone. Many years ago, one of us had a dispute with an editor who changed the word "said" to "claimed," following a source's quote. From the writer's point of view, the editor's word choice signaled suspicion about the information the source was conveying. This was an unintended message, and the writer's preference for "said" prevailed.

AVOID PASSIVE VOICE

As Hamilton College's Writing Center explains, "Passive voice produces a sentence in which the subject *receives* an action. In contrast, active voice produces a sentence in which the subject *performs* an action."[12]

The Writing Center provides some good examples of the ways in which active voice "creates clearer more concise sentences," while passive voice is less direct and often wordier:

Passive: My first trip abroad will always be remembered by me.

Active: I will always remember my first trip abroad.

Passive: On April 19, 1775, arms were seized by British soldiers at Concord, precipitating the American Revolution.

Active: On April 19, 1775, British soldiers seized arms at Concord, precipitating the American Revolution.

Passive: Thomas Jefferson's support of the new Constitution was documented in a letter to James Madison.

Active: Thomas Jefferson documented his support of the new Constitution in a letter to James Madison.[13]

Passive voice takes the wind out of your sails because it creates uncertainty about just who is doing what, and that waters down your verb.

There is one exception to this rule: you might intentionally want to hide the actor in a sentence to avoid embarrassing someone or to disguise a political player—for example, "The bill was passed last night." You might want to use the passive if there are difficult negotiations, and several key votes came in at the last minute. You might not want to call out someone whose support could cause trouble back in the home district. The key here is that, when using passive voice, it should be intentional—not sloppy or inadvertent or both.

We've occasionally caught ourselves doing just this when we're insecure about the facts in something we're writing. When we edit ourselves, we recognize that if we're not sure about an idea, we shouldn't say it altogether rather than just confusing matters.

SELECT QUOTATIONS JUDICIOUSLY

Using quotes from other authors' works is a useful technique to make writing lively. But when you can say something better yourself than the person you're quoting, rely on your own words. Think of quotes as the salt on an order of French fries. Just the right amount is delicious, but with too much, the fries can be inedible. If it's important to attribute facts to a source, then it's easy to paraphrase much of the thought and then use a short quote to top it off, as *Stateline* does here:

> "Maine schools rarely serve fresh fish, even though Maine is a coastal state, because of the cost," said Robin Kerber, coordinator of the state's Farm and Sea to School program. The high cost also means many children may not see fresh fish on their dinner plates and don't know whether they like it. "There are a lot of communities where the parents are fishermen or lobstermen, but the family can't afford to eat it," she said in an interview.[14]

Sometimes quotes are particularly powerful when they're used to end a paragraph with a punch. Consider this from a column by Peter Coy in the *New York Times*:

> Rhonda Vonshay Sharpe, the founder and president of the Women's Institute for Science Equity and Race, told me that social media is focusing attention on longstanding gaps in wealth, making people more sensitive to issues of money. "Everybody's life looks fabulous through the social media filters," she said.[15]

Fortunately, the use of hyperlinks makes it possible to refer back to a lengthier quotation from which you can draw a small amount. When you need to demonstrate that you've mastered the background literature in a field, you can summarize the main ideas and then provide citations for the relevant literature you've relied on. Your summary can be an important, original contribution that is best made without quoting everyone who has written on a subject.

CHOOSE SHORT, PUNGENT WORDS

Short words can be more powerful than multisyllabic ones (particularly those that are jargon). Bigger words don't necessarily mean you're more intelligent. The convincing evidence of that comes from writing good sentences, not from packing big words into the sentence.

Anglo-Saxon words often fit this category. As Turner Ink writes,

> Why choose Anglo Saxon words over Latin? They seem a bit crude compared to the flowery elegance of Latin-derived words. Well, they are. But Anglo-Saxon words also tend to be shorter, punchier, and more direct; whereas Latin words tend to be longer and more abstract.[16]

Here are a few examples: instead of using the word "miniscule," use "puny"; instead of "parsimonious," use "cheap" or "thrifty"; instead of "incinerate," use "burn." One caution: more unusual words stand out in prose, and so it's wise to avoid turning to the same punchy word more than once in the same piece.

That's the art of writing a lively concerto that your audience will remember.

FROM OUR KEYBOARDS

From a 1991 Barrett and Greene feature about management capacity in America's thirty largest cities in *Financial World* magazine: "Like wrinkled grandmothers sitting in a nursing home solarium, many of America's old cities seem able to do little more than complain about their aches and pains and wonder why their old friends have stopped visiting."[17]

NOTES

1. Eric Larson, *The Splendid and the Vile: A Saga of Churchill, Family and Defiance During the Blitz* (New York: Crown, 2020).

2. Larson, *The Splendid and the Vile.*

3. David Stanway, "Rising Antarctic Ice Melt Will Dramatically Slow Glacial Water Flows, Study Finds," Reuters, March 29, 2023, https://www.reuters.com/business/environment/rising-antarctic-ice-melt-will-dramatically-slow-global-ocean-flows-study-2023-03-29/.

4. Leo Tolstoy, *Anna Karenina,* trans. Constance Garnett, chapter 1, https://www.gutenberg.org/ebooks/1399.

5. "10 Ways to Grow as a Songwriter and Write Better Songs," *Ninebuzz Music Apps* (blog), December 2, 2021, https://ninebuzz.com/10-ways-to-grow-as-a-songwriter-and-write-better-songs/.

6. Matt Ellis, "The Ultimate Guide to Paragraphs," *Grammarly* (blog), February 22, 2021, https://www.grammarly.com/blog/paragraphs/?gclid=Cj0KCQiAgaGgBhC8ARIsAAAyLfFp71wmVjNmnu63rCmeUTuAjNlfjSHRv0WTMoEzNnvYOdUCyd3VwXAaApH6EALw_wcB&gclsrc=aw.ds (accessed November 2, 2023).

7. "Paragraphs," The Writing Center, University of North Carolina, https://writingcenter.unc.edu/tips-and-tools/paragraphs (accessed November 2, 2023).

8. "Paragraphing," Open House, https://warwick.ac.uk/fac/soc/al/globalpad-rip/openhouse/academicenglishskills/writing/paragraphing/.

9. William Shakespeare, *Romeo and Juliet,* Act 2, Scene 2

10. Jason Collins, "Abstract or Too Abstract: The Use of Metaphor and Analogy in Academic Writing," *Impactio* (blog), January 27, 2021, https://www.impactio.com/blog/abstract-or-too-abstract-the-use-of-metaphor-and-analogy-in-academic-writing (accessed November 2, 2023).

11. "What are Powerful Verbs," EdPlace, https://www.edplace.com/blog/edplace-explains/what-are-powerful-verbs (accessed November 2, 2023).

12. "Passive Voice," Hamilton, https://www.hamilton.edu/academics/centers/writing/seven-sins-of-writing/1.

13. "Passive Voice," Hamilton.

14. Marsha Mercer, "Carrots for Carrots: States Promote Buying Local for School Lunches," *Stateline*, September 30, 2022, https://stateline.org/2022/09/30/carrots-for-carrots-states-promote-buying-local-for-school-lunches/.

15. Peter Coy, "Money Is Up. Patriotism and Religion Are Down," *New York Times*, March 29, 2023, https://www.nytimes.com/2023/03/29/opinion/money-is-up-patriotism-and-religion-are-down.html.

16. "Why Anglo Saxon Rules (in Business Writing Anyway)," *Turner Ink* (blog), April 24, 2009, https://www.turnerink.co.uk/copywriting/using-anglo-saxon-words/#:~:text =So%20why%20choose%20Anglo%20Saxon,be%20longer%20and%20more%20abstract.

17. Katherine Barrett and Richard Greene, "American Cities: A Special Report," *Financial World*, February 19, 1991, 24.

Chapter 5

Shoot for the Target

Keep Your Writing at the Appropriate Length

Back in 2008, a query came into WritersWeekly.com asking about the importance of writing an article to the precise length prescribed by a publisher. The answer was to the point:

> One of the stressful parts of print publishing is that each article must fit into a specific, pre-assigned spot in a magazine/newspaper. Going over or under by only 20 words can seriously impact the end-result of the layout of that entire page. So, when an editor says 1000 words, they mean 1000 words. While I would say 999 words or 1001 words would probably go undetected, to stay in high favor with an editor and to land future assignments, give them 1000. If you don't cut it, the editor will need to fix it and, trust me, they hate that. You know your article better than anybody and you are the one best suited to cut/add material.[1]

That guidance remains powerful. Even though many publications (especially those that are exclusively online) give a leeway of more than a small handful of words, shooting for the target is always wise advice—not necessarily easy but wise.

This advice, moreover, applies not just to blogs and short-form pieces. Most academic journals have page or word limits. If you write long—and for academics, that tends to be more likely than coming in short—you might face a quick rejection from the editor or a harrumph from reviewers. In books, editors have done a careful calculation of the costs of your book based on the number of words you're proposing to write. Coming in too short risks having the editor decide that your work isn't as thorough as expected. Coming in long can throw off the financial calculations behind the decision to offer a contract.

In all these cases, length limits exist for a reason. Smart writers don't tempt fate by ignoring those limits.

We turned to the editors of *PA Times*, the publication of the American Society for Public Administration, to ask about the word count for its articles, which we knew to be 850. The publication allows for a little leeway, but if a piece comes in at over 900 words, they'll send it back to the author to shorten it. Why are they so stringent? According to the *PA Times* editors,

> Our word count policy is based on the limited attention span online readers have for the articles they're scanning. Good online articles must be interesting from the start, avoid jargon and end concisely in order to keep readers' attention. . . . Ultimately, this policy is good for the author and the audience.[2]

KEEP CONTROL OF YOUR WRITING

PA Times' policy of sending articles back to authors for shortening may seem like a pain in the neck, but it's the height of generosity. The alternative for editors is to simply cut the piece to length themselves—or reject it completely. Their opinion about what is truly important may differ dramatically from that of the writer. The editor's yielding control over those decisions can be frustrating for an author. Smart writers try to ensure that the message they want to send is the one that survives through the editing and production process.

What's more, when editors cut copy to length, they can easily lose the nuances that readers know are important for accuracy. You may, for example, have written a sentence like this: "When

Figure 5.1. Source: Getty Images, Creative #6803338102; credit: Getty Images/Lamaip.

outspoken opponents of the legislation aren't given the opportunity to advocate for their cause, there's little chance they'll ever buy in." An editor, seeking to get that twenty-two-word sentence down, could rewrite it as "When people aren't given the opportunity to advocate for their cause, they won't buy in." (See textbox 5.1.)

The second sentence sounds a whole lot like the first one, and it's seven words shorter. But if you were referring exclusively to outspoken opponents of the legislation about which you're writing, the new, shorter version misses the point. So perhaps you should have written the sentence like this: "Outspoken opponents of the legislation may buy in if they can promote their cause." That's a little shorter than the editor's version, and it communicates what you intended to say.

We suggested back in chapter 2 that you talk to your dog as an approach to writing clear, cogent prose. The same advice holds for writing to length. If you read a piece aloud to a colleague, a friend, or even your dog, you'll often take note of sentences that ramble and points that could easily be left out. Of course, your dog might be more generous.

TEXTBOX 5.1. THE LONG AND SHORT OF IT

Following is a paragraph that runs forty-six words, followed by the same paragraph, which we've cut by more than half. As you'll see, no vital facts have been lost, and the second version reads better than the first.

Long Version (forty-six words): "Meanwhile, while the city of London was fighting the dreadful pandemic, its population could hardly stop debating whether or not masks were necessary to cut down on the spread of this dread disease, before it sucked the vitality out of the citizens of England's largest city."

Shorter, Better Version (eighteen words): "While London fought the pandemic, people there raucously debated how effectively masks limit the spread of the disease."

In a sentence or paragraph, fewer words are almost always better than more words. Readers like snappy prose. And fewer words avoid the problem that Emperor Joseph II complained about in the movie *Amadeus*. Mozart had just premiered *The Abduction from the Seraglio*, which the emperor had commissioned. The emperor, however, wasn't pleased when he heard the opera. "There simply are too many notes," he said.[3] No writer wants to be dismissed because a piece has, well, too many notes.

TIPS FOR WRITING EFFECTIVELY TO LENGTH

It's not always easy squeezing all your good ideas into a limited amount of space. Here are some techniques that will help.

Concrete examples are great, but they can be overused. Real-world examples can liven up your writing and clarify the idea. But you can cut back your word count by using only the best example, not all you can conjure.

Listen to Ernest Hemingway's advice, and "kill your babies."[4] That great American novelist wasn't talking about infanticide, but about writing as tightly and straightforwardly as possible by editing out material that you have come to love. Face it: editing your own work can be painful—especially when you've worked hard to come up with dozens of facts, anecdotes, ideas, and points. But you're not doing the reader (or your editor) any service when you feel obliged to cram them all in. Writing—and then editing—from the point of view of the reader is essential. Falling so much in love with your own words that you can't bear to cut them can cause big problems.

Consider cutting the first paragraph out entirely (or, at least, checking to see what the introduction looks like without it). Often an effort to set up the thesis for a piece of writing can consist of a great deal of excessive verbiage that doesn't engage the reader (and a quick time-out—doesn't this sentence strike you as an example of excessive verbiage?). Many writers use the first paragraph as a form of throat clearing that doesn't really advance the argument. And some writers don't know what they really want to say at the beginning until they get to the end. No matter the form in which you're writing—book, article, blog, op-ed, or some other publication—think carefully, when you get to the end, about how you want to begin.

Minimize the use of unnecessary words to lead into transitions. To make a piece seem like it flows smoothly, there's a temptation to begin sentences with words like "in the meantime," "naturally," and "certainly." Such words can often be eliminated without any loss to the reader. Valerie Fridland lays out the importance of these points in her book *Like, Literally, Dude: Arguing for the Good in Bad Language.*[5]

Seek out redundancies and see if thoughts can be combined to make the same point in a more concise way. No one likes to read the same idea twice (like this second sentence, which repeats the point in the first).

Use beautiful adjectives and powerful adverbs judiciously. If we wanted to get some words out of the preceding sentence, we'd have written "Use adjectives and adverbs judiciously," and that's the point of this tip. While descriptive words can help make your writing intriguing and vivid, they can easily be overused. Pick the best one, use it, and often, that's enough.

If you pick descriptive words carefully, you rarely need to use the word "very" to make them seem stronger. Say you want to add the word "very" to happy to make someone "very happy." Instead, consider changing "happy" to "joyous," and you'll get to the same place but with more powerful, shorter writing. (And by the way, never use the word "very" to describe something that's "unique." Unique is, well, unique, and it can't be a halfway point.)

FROM OUR KEYBOARDS

In a report written by two of us for the Volcker Alliance, we wrote the following: "On the positive side, unlike prior years, Alabama avoided deferring recurring expenditures into future years." Our editor insisted in angry red letters, "Let's not use up precious space with throat-clearing transitions" and cut out the four words "On the positive side." He was right. Those words were unnecessary.

NOTES

1. "How Strict Are Word Counts in Articles," WritersWeekly.com, Ask the Expert, published February 13, 2008, https://writersweekly.com/ask -the-expert/how-strict-are-word-counts-in-articles.

2. Email to the authors, March 31, 2023.

3. IMDB, *Amadeus* (1984), https://www.imdb.com/title/tt0086879/ characters/nm0001371 (accessed November 2, 2023).

4. Quoted by J. M. Frey, "Words for Writers: Killing Your Babies," March 1, 2012, https://jmfrey.net/2012/03/killing-your-babies.

5. Valerie Fridland, *Like, Literally, Dude: Arguing for the Good in Bad English* (New York: Viking Press, 2023).

Chapter 6

A Picture Is Worth a Thousand Words

Visualize Your Data to Communicate Complex Facts Clearly

Experts date the origin of this chapter's title to the early 1900s.[1] Some say it was the product of an advertising executive, Frederick R. Barnard. In 1921 he titled a piece in *Printer's Ink* about graphics in advertising with "One Look Is Worth a Thousand Words"; then in 1927, the trade magazine used the phrase again, changing it to "Chinese Proverb: One Picture Is Worth Ten Thousand Words."[2]

As far as we can tell, the actual existence of a Chinese proverb is questionable. (See chapter 7, which deals with the challenge of figuring out what's true.) But even if the facts are a bit squishy, at its heart, the concept is sound. Both photographs and artwork distill complex ideas in a way that readers are likely to remember. The drawings on the wall by cave dwellers more than thirty-five thousand years ago were early infographics.[3]

Back then, conveying thoughts in pictures was the only option. There was no written language. But even with some 470,000 entries in *Webster's Third New International Dictionary* (unabridged), infographics—including graphs, charts, tables, and more—are powerful tools for making those words come to life in a vivid and comprehensible fashion. Public relations and digital marketing firm Comprise puts it this way:

> Infographics tell a story in a snapshot. Information can be overwhelming or boring when it's displayed in a long block of text, infographics help the most important facts stand out. By breaking up a long piece of text with icons and other graphic elements, the information becomes more visually interesting. Done right, data visualizations will catch viewers' eyes and make them more likely to remember the information than if they had just read it in a page of text. Also, infographics are made for sharing. We are living in the age of social media. Attention spans are shrinking, and more people are likely to look at an infographic than read a full article.[4]

TELLING AN UNFORGETTABLE STORY

It's possible that your high school or college history courses didn't teach you much about Napoleon's disastrous invasion of Russia in 1812. He made it to Moscow, but the city was deserted. He stayed for four months, hoping to convince the Russians to sue for peace. That never happened, and facing horrific weather, he retreated to France. Along the way, Russian guerillas—and the bitter cold—exacted a terrible price. Napoleon set off with an army of 422,000 soldiers. He returned with just 10,000.

Was it a remarkable historic event? Of course. But if you really want to get a feeling for it in ways that words can't capture, take one look at the chart (figure 6.1) that was prepared in 1869 by French graphic designer Charles-Joseph Minard.[5]

The chart accomplishes three remarkable feats. First, it captures the story of one of the largest military defeats in history. Second, it stimulates interest in a moment of history because it makes further reading about this war irresistible. Third, it creates an inescapable memory. Great pictures frame the world in ways that can't be forgotten. In fact, one of the very best experts on data visualization,

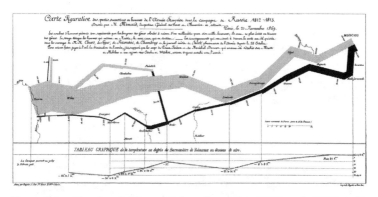

Figure 6.1. Napoleon's Disastrous Invasion, 1812. Source: Charles-Joseph Minard, Carte figurative des pertes successives en hommes de l'Armée Francais dans la campagne de Russe 1812–1813, https://sciencenorway .no/blog-blog-from-numbers-to-graphics-statistics/charles-joseph-minards -map-of-napoleons-flawed-russian-campaign-an-ever-current-classic /1618695.

Edward Tufte, says that Minard's chart is "probably the best statistical graphic ever drawn."[6]

The 422,000 soldiers he began with are represented by the lighter, thick line that moves from left to right on the graphic. That line shows the loss of three-fourths of his troops on the rugged trip to Moscow. Following the black line from right to left again, you can see what happened to his troops on the way back. You can almost feel the biting cold and heavy snow as the line gets narrower and narrower and culminates with a representation of the 2 percent of the troops who set out and lived to return home.

CREATE PICTURES FOR YOUR WORDS

Some academic papers are a real slog—so much so that researchers have even developed hints for reading papers you don't understand.[7] (If the authors of those papers had used this book, we'd like to think these hints wouldn't be necessary).

One guide from the National Institutes of Medicine, in fact, makes a point that applies to all academic papers. It points out that "some people like to scrutinize the figures and tables (including legends) before reading any of the main text."[8]

There are lots of computer programs that work well for visualizing data, including Microsoft Excel and Google Charts. There is also a large and growing collection of artificial intelligence tools that can create a chart about virtually anything. But the many options for drawing charts increase the risk of confusing, not persuading, your readers. Bad charts that attempt to display good data can sabotage efforts to engage readers with insights.

What steps should you use in preparing effective graphs and charts? We asked the artificial intelligence engine ChatGPT for tips. Elsewhere in this book, we caution readers that they shouldn't trust chatbots to be accurate. But in this instance, the computer spat out some very sensible pieces of advice:

Here are some AI tips for drawing effective graphs and charts:

- *Know your audience*: Consider who will be looking at your graph or chart, and tailor it to their needs. Think about the level of detail and the type of data that they would find useful.
- *Keep it simple*: Your graph or chart should be easy to read and understand. Avoid clutter and unnecessary details. Use clear labels and titles. (See figure 6.2 for example.)
- *Choose the right type of graph or chart*: Different types of data require different types of graphs or charts. Bar graphs are good for comparing values, line graphs are good for showing trends over time, and pie charts are good for showing proportions.
- *Use appropriate scales*: Make sure the scale you use is appropriate for the data you are presenting. For example, if you are showing data that ranges from 0 to 100, don't use a scale that goes from 0 to 1,000.
- *Use colors effectively*: Use colors to draw attention to important information, but don't use too many colors or use colors that are too similar.

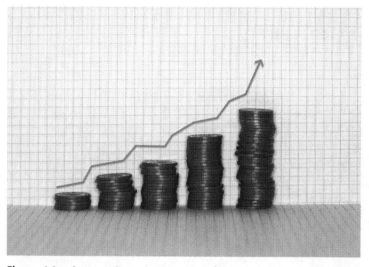

Figure 6.2. Source: Getty Images, Creative #92601377; credit: Getty Images/carlp778.

- *Keep it visually appealing*: Use good design principles to make your graph or chart visually appealing. Use a clear font and layout and avoid distracting backgrounds or images.
- *Test your graph or chart*: Before using your graph or chart, test it on a few people to make sure it is easy to read and understand. Make any necessary adjustments before sharing it with a wider audience.

A particularly important tip is the last one. Try your data visualization out on friends, research colleagues, and mentors. Ask them these basic questions: What does the visualization show? Is it crystal clear? Is the figure worth a thousand words?

PAINT THE RIGHT PICTURE

While graphics are powerful communication devices, there are a number of traps to avoid in selecting them.

Don't use too many pictures. After all, the phrase isn't "Ten pictures are worth ten thousand words." Overuse of graphs, charts, and tables can diminish the power of all of them. How many are too many? Don't think about how many pictures you can produce or whether you ought to use all the charts you can make, no matter how much you love them. Rather, think about your biggest ideas, which typically wouldn't be more than a handful in a paper or a chapter of a book—and then use infographics for each.

Don't overreach. A reporter on a local news station presented a story on the increase in crime, focusing on what he said was a 50 percent increase in murders. The graph that was used showed a 50 percent increase—from four murders to six. In this case, neither the graph nor the argument about a 50 percent increase was meaningful.

Don't game the graphs. Skillful graph drawers know how to game their charts to punch up the theme they want to emphasize. Some novices stumble into that problem inadvertently. For example, if an author wants to emphasize the growth in government spending, it can be tempting to set the y-axis (the vertical part of the line) at a place that maximizes the gap on the chart between this year's spending and last year's. This is a time-honored technique, and it's one that authors are often tempted to use. If a reader suspects an author of trickery, that can lower the reader's confidence in other parts of the author's data. Doug Jones, Kansas City, Missouri's auditor, offers this explanation for an article that two of us wrote about data quality.

When the scale of a chart changes, the appearance of the data can communicate entirely different messages. A chart that shows numbers on a scale of 1 to 100, for example, may make a 3–5 percent change seem tiny. But if the chart only goes up to 30, that 3–5 percent change can look extremely dramatic.[9]

FROM OUR KEYBOARDS

In a report on the lessons to remember from the COVID crisis, we worked to summarize our findings and, especially, to identify which level of government needed to work on which problems. We titled our chart "Rudolph's Nose," conjuring a pleasant visual

Rudolph's Nose

No individual team member can ever pull the weight of solving a complex problem. In many complex situations, however, one team member needs to take the lead. That is the lesson of Rudolph and Santa's reindeer. On an especially foggy night, Santa needed Rudolph's special talents to guide his sleigh. The lessons of COVID teach the same lesson. When dealing with crises, responsibility is sometimes spread evenly across all levels of government. To meet some challenges, however, multiple levels of government need to be involved—even when one player often needs to guide the sleigh—as the following figure shows.

	Federal	State	Local
1. Remember all crises are local		●	●
2. Frame central policy to build local support	●		
3. Establish data as a language	●		
4. Coordinate goods, services, and logistics	●		
5. Grow the experts we need	●	●	●
6. Use artificial intelligence and create predictive analytics	●		
7. Manage risks		●	●
8. Build networks	●	●	●
9. Earn trust	●	●	●
10. Learn from the "laboratories of democracy"	●		
11. Ensure that accountability isn't a casualty of crisis	●	●	●
12. Pursue equity as prime goal	●	●	●

Figure 6.3. Rudolph's Nose. Source: From "Managing the Next Crisis: Twelve Principles for Dealing with Viral Uncertainty," authored by Barrett, Greene, and Kettl.

image for readers. The chart itself (see figure 6.3) served a very simple purpose of showing the diverse roles of all the government players who, together, need to get the job done.[10]

NOTES

1. "A Picture is Worth a Thousand Words," The Idioms, https://www.theidioms.com/a-picture-is-worth-a-thousand-words (accessed November 1, 2023).

2. "A Picture Is Worth a Thousand Words," The Phrase Finder, https://www.phrases.org.uk/meanings/a-picture-is-worth-a-thousand-words.html (accessed November 1, 2023).

3. Jo Marchant, "A Journey to the Oldest Cave Paintings in the World," *Smithsonian Magazine*, January 2016, https://www.smithsonianmag.com/history/journey-oldest-cave-paintings-world-180957685.

4. "Why Infographics Are Useful," Comprise, https://comprise.agency/our-thoughts/why-infographics-are-useful (accessed November 1, 2023).

5. Sara Brinch, "Charles-Joseph Minard's Map of Napolean's Flawed Russian Campaign: An Ever-Current Classic," *From Numbers to Graphics* (blog), *Sciencenorway.no*, March 22, 2019, https://sciencenorway.no/blog-blog-from-numbers-to-graphics-statistics/charles-joseph-minards-map-of-napoleons-flawed-russian-campaign-an-ever-current-classic/1618695.

6. "Poster: Napoleon's March," Edwardtufte.com, https://www.edwardtufte.com/tufte/posters (accessed November 1, 2023).

7. For hints, see Tyasning Kroemer, "How to Read and Understand Hard Scientific Papers," Gold Biotechnology, https://goldbio.com/articles/article/how-to-read-and-understand-hard-scientific-papers (accessed November 1, 2023); For reading papers you don't understand, see Adam Ruben, "How to (Seriously) Read a Scientific Paper," *Science*, March 21, 2016, https://www.science.org/content/article/how-seriously-read-scientific-paper.

8. Maureen A. Carey, Kevin L. Steiner, and William A. Petri, Jr., "Ten Simple Rules for Reading a Scientific Paper," *National Library of Medicine* 16, no. 7 (July 30, 2020): e1008032, https://www.ncbi.nlm.nih.gov/pmc/articles/PMC7392212.

9. Katherine Barrett and Richard Greene, "Data-Based Decision-Making Is Flawed When the Data Is Flawed," *Route Fifty*, March 2, 2023, https:

//www.route-fifty.com/digital-government/2023/03/data-based-decision-making-flawed-when-data-flawed/383539.

10. Katherine Barrett, Richard Greene, and Donald F. Kettl, "Managing the Next Crisis: Twelve Principles for Dealing with Viral Uncertainty," IBM Center for the Business of Government, published 2021, 43, https://www.businessofgovernment.org/sites/default /files/ Managing%20the%20Next%20Crisis_0.pdf.

Chapter 7

"All We Want Are the Facts, Ma'am"

Make Sure There's Evidence to Support Your Argument

Through the 1950s one of the two major characters in the very popular television show *Dragnet* was Sgt. Joe Friday, played by actor Jack Webb. He was a taciturn, monosyllabic cop who couldn't waste his time with female suspects who were talking too much for his pleasure. Out of that grew the catchphrase "Just the facts, ma'am," which is what people believed he frequently said to the women he interrogated. We've heard that line over and over, and originally, it seemed like an ideal title for this chapter.

Then we did a little fact-checking.

According to award-winning website Shmoop, which delves into the origins of famous quotes, "he never said those exact words! The closest he came was 'All we want are the facts, ma'am.'"[1]

This struck us as quite an irony as the point of this chapter is to stress the importance of ensuring accuracy in anything you write and to provide some time-tested techniques for fact-checking.

Of course, everyone remembers the famous line from *Star Wars: The Empire Strikes Back*, when Darth Vader says to Luke Skywalker, "Luke, I am your father." Except, as it turns out, he never says it. What Darth Vader actually says is "No, I am your father."[2]

People who are trained in an academic way of writing are generally extremely careful about their facts—and often footnote each and every one of them (and sometimes everyone who has ever written about each fact). But when they try to broaden their audience to have greater impact and enter a realm that's more like traditional journalism, surprisingly simple errors can crop up—like the incorrect spelling of a source's name or an incorrect title.

ACCURACY IS THE KEY TO CREDIBILITY

According to Lee E. Krahenbuhl, coordinator of the Communications Studies Program at Stevenson University, "whether you are a journalist, researcher, writer or someone in the professional fields, it is important to know how to identify real information and use it accurately. That's our real challenge in the 21st century."[3] That's even more the case with the rise of

Figure 7.1. Source: Getty Images, Creative #1182934020; credit: Getty Images/filo.

AI-assisted writing, where the technology is only as accurate as the web sources it draws on.

Whatever you're writing, a certain portion of your audience is going to know something about the topic. Experts, who are often the people in a position to translate the major findings of your prose into real-world action, are going to be suspicious the moment they can identify a factual error.

Consider the article on the front page of the *New York Times* on March 31, 2023, about Mississippi's rejection of federal funding for health insurance for the poor. It stated that nearly 35 percent of residents of the Mississippi Delta are Black. The truth is that the number is about two-thirds. At least the *Times* issued a correction when the error was discovered.[4] (In fact, the *Times* has a special section on its website devoted to correcting errors that appear in print.)

But for a portion of the *Times'* readership who are familiar with the Delta, this simple error likely cast doubt on any of the other information provided in the article. If a reader discovers a single error, there's no reason that the reader should believe anything else in the article—even though the remainder may be entirely right. That's an opportunity lost.

The Lloyd Sealy Library at the John Jay College of Criminal Justice at the City University of New York presents some "facts" that are frequently published inaccurately:

- numbers and statistics (mixing up "billions" and "millions")
- names of people, titles, locations
- ages
- historical facts
- superlatives like "only," "first" and "most"
- dates[5]

BEWARE THE INTERNET

As people become increasingly reliant on the internet to gather information, they put themselves at risk of picking up questionable material. That's why it's critical to take great care with the websites from which you are getting information. There are several steps that writers can take to help avoid picking up mistakes from online sources:

Consider the funding that may lead to biases in research. One PhD student of our acquaintance found an online article written under the auspices of a national think tank. It indicated that when children used different kinds of building blocks to develop spatial learning, they were more inclined to get jobs in science, technology, engineering, and mathematics fields. But when she dug further, she discovered that the research had been funded by a giant, well-known manufacturer of children's construction sets. That doesn't mean this research was inaccurate or influenced by bias, but when a funder has skin in the game, it's a red flag that signals the wisdom of finding another source for the same conclusions.

Be wary of headlines. Since the main measure of success of writing online is the number of readers who click on the item, there's a powerful temptation to use the strongest, harshest, most inflammatory words in the headline, even if the article doesn't support them. A friend of ours who worked for a large, nationally known, information-providing website had the job of updating headlines on stories over the course of the day to make them stronger and stronger if not enough clicks were coming in. The stories were the same—it was the headlines that changed. Major newspapers often rotate stories on and off their home page based on these clicks, and jazzing up the headlines can be an important way of drawing new readers. (See figure 7.2 for an example.)

Don't rely on Wikipedia. While this online encyclopedia is a terrific source of information and its corps of volunteer editors are careful about adjusting entries to make sure they're accurate, mistakes can still creep in. According to Scribber.com,

There's some disagreement about whether Wikipedia can be considered a reliable source. Because it can be edited by anyone, many people argue that it's easy for misleading information to be added to an article without the reader knowing. Others argue that because Wikipedia articles cite their sources, and because they are worked on by so many editors, misinformation is generally removed quickly. However, most universities state that you shouldn't cite Wikipedia in your writing.[6]

Most of all, beware of opulently false information that can appear on the internet—especially on social media like Facebook. A couple of years ago, for example, a post went viral that says, "After years of telling people chemotherapy is the only way to try and eliminate cancer, Johns Hopkins is finally starting to tell you there is an alternative way."[7] It went on to make claims that

Figure 7.2.   Source: Getty Images, Creative #471330049; credit: DNY59.

Johns Hopkins advocates a diet that is better than chemo for treating cancer.

The university responded by pointing out that this myth had been around since 2004, writing that "Johns Hopkins did not publish the information, which often is an email attachment, nor do we endorse its contents."[8]

CHATBOTS MAKE MISTAKES TOO (LOTS OF THEM)

Enthralled by the potential of artificial intelligence to answer every question under the sun through a growing array of chatbots, there's a strong temptation for writers to rely on them. In fact, this remarkable new technology may be even more seductive than the internet because it doesn't require scouring through the articles provided by a search engine to find information.

It's likely that these devices will improve over time, but it's unlikely that they'll be infallible sources of information anytime soon. When we were finishing up work on this chapter in July 2023, we asked an AI-based bot, "What books did John F. Kennedy write?"

Its answer began, "John F. Kennedy, the 35th President of the United States was a prolific writer, but he did not publish any books during his lifetime. Instead, he authored several works that were posthumously published. The most well-known and influential of these works is *Profiles in Courage*, for which Kennedy won the Pulitzer Prize in 1957."

What gibberish. *Profiles in Courage* did indeed win the Pulitzer Prize in 1957, but of course, Kennedy wasn't assassinated until 1963, so he was very much available to accept the Pulitzer Prize. (Incidentally, there's ample evidence that even when Kennedy was alive, the book was ghostwritten for him by his aide Theodore C. Sorenson.)

IT'S YOUR RESPONSIBILITY

Rare is the editor who has the time to fact-check articles that you submit, and since it's your name on the piece, it's your credibility and reputation that's ultimately at stake. That's why it's important to be certain that anything you write is 100 percent accurate (see textbox 7.1).

It might seem that the easiest part of this process is to check the spelling and titles of individuals. Why not just go to LinkedIn or a respected website? The answer is that both can easily be wrong.

TEXTBOX 7.1. QUESTIONS TO ASK YOURSELF

Following are tips from Barbara Gray, associate professor and chief librarian of the CUNY Graduate School of Journalism, about how to start a good fact-checking process. She suggests that you consider the following:

- Who says?
  - Scrutinize the publication sharing the story and the sources they are quoting. Are they even giving a source?
  - Check the "About Us" page or whoxy.com for domain registry info.

- How do they know?
  - Have you heard of them? What makes them an authoritative source for anything?

- Are they biased?
  - Does the story only present one side of a debate?
  - Look for them on sourcewatch.org.

- Does this news turn up on any trusted site?
  - Search to see whether or how the news is being reported on legitimate journalism sites (but be wary of mistaking quantity for quality—fake news tends to proliferate).

- What don't I know?
  - What facts are being left out? Do other reliable sources challenge these facts?[9]

People who don't often use LinkedIn can let their biographical information go out of date. The person might have moved on to an entirely different position.

Using biographies you can find on the internet—even on very credible sites—can also lead you astray. For example, if you were trying to find information about two of the authors of this book and looked at the website for the Fels Institute at the University of Pennsylvania in summer 2023, you'd find that "the husband-and-wife team are senior fellows at the Fels Institute of Government at the University of Pennsylvania."

That was true once, but it hasn't been since 2017. (The error has since been corrected.)

Since even the simplest of facts can't easily be validated on the internet, it's generally a good idea to make direct contact with the source of the information you're using (and, of course, there must be a source of some sort—otherwise you're just picking up something you've heard may be true, and that's a writing hazard).

Sources are generally agreeable about working with you to double-check information. They don't want you to get something wrong any more than you do, especially if it's about them. You can do this by email, phone, or text.

The key is to keep careful track of each and every fact in everything you write and make sure that it's accurate before it goes to an editor. For shorter pieces of writing, this is easily done by underlining each item (either manually or electronically) and, once it's checked, recording the source.

Browser plug-ins, like Project Fib, B.S. Detector, Media Bias Fact Check, and StopTheBullS#!t, also claim to find problems of fact. But there's nothing like checking the facts yourself and then annotating them with a hyperlink or a highlight on your screen.

The least complicated part of this process is fact-checking information that you've taken directly from a document. It's easy to make a mistake with a piece of data you've gotten from a survey, study, dissertation, or database. So it's always a good plan to go back to the original source and compare number to number and fact to fact. Then attribute accordingly, and you're probably on safe ground.

One warning: Sometimes definitions contained in published data can be confusing and complex. There's a temptation to simplify, but when you do that, you may be imprecise and misrepresent the original research. So unless you're drawing the verbiage verbatim from the original document, don't hesitate to reach out to the author for clarification.

For example, the Census Bureau's numbers can sometimes require explanation. The folks who work there are only too happy to help confirm that you've understood their meaning correctly. We've often been surprised by the personal replies we've received from the staff at Census.

And here is one additional tip: tag your facts with the sources as you write with a footnote, endnote, or hyperlink. It's much easier to do that upfront rather than after you've finished drafting and need to recall where you found a particular piece of information.

FROM OUR KEYBOARDS

From a Barrett and Greene B&G Report in January 2023: A column was written and put online titled "Eight New Governors and a Generational Shift." It included a list of the new governors elected in November 2022. The piece ended with an allegedly helpful list of the new heads of the states. A few hours later, while rereading the piece, one of the team discovered that the new governor of Arkansas had been left out, and the title had to be changed to mention "Nine New Governors." Fortunately, that one was caught before a note came in from the state of Arkansas wondering what had happened to Governor Sarah Huckabee Sanders.[10]

NOTES

1. "Dragnet Quotes," Shmoop, https://www.shmoop.com/quotes/just -the-facts-maam.html (accessed November 2, 2023).

2. Claire Nowak, "15 Famous Movie Quotes Everyone Gets Wrong," *Reader's Digest*, March 7, 2023, https://www.rd.com/list/movie-quotes -everyone-gets-wrong/.

3. "How to Identify Reliable Information," Stevenson University Online, https://www.stevenson.edu/online/about-us/news/how-to -identify-reliable-information (accessed November 2, 2023).

4. "Corrections: March 31, 2023," *New York Times*, https://www .nytimes.com/2023/03/30/pageoneplus/corrections-march-31-2023.html (last updated August 21, 2019).

5. Brian Carroll, "Fact Checking, Verification & Fake News," Lloyd Sealy Library, updated August 21, 2019, https://guides.lib.jjay.cuny.edu /c.php?g=618074&p=4300847.

6. "Frequently Asked Questions: Is Wikipedia a Reliable Source for Academic Research?" Scribbr, https://www.scribbr.com/frequently -asked-questions/is-wikipedia-a-reliable-source (accessed November 2, 2023)..

7. McKenzie Sadeghi, "Fact Check: 'Cancer Update' Claiming to Come from Johns Hopkins Hospital Is a Hoax," *USA Today*, March 10, 2021, https://www.usatoday.com/story/news/factcheck/2021/03/10/fact -check-cancer-update-claiming-johns-hopkins-hoax/4608962001.

8. Sadeghi, "Fact Check."

9. Barbara Gray, "10 Tips for Fighting Fake News: How to Fact Check Like a Pro," lexisnexis.com, 2017, https://www.lexisnexis.com/pdf/nexis /Nexis-webinar-how-to-fact-check-like-a-pro.pdf.

10. Katherine Barrett and Richard Greene, "Nine New Governors and a Generational Shift," *B&G Report*, January 5, 2023.

Chapter 8

Don't Forget Your Pitchfork

Learn How to Make the Best Possible Argument for the Pieces You Are Writing through a Pitch That Engages Your Readers

You've been working hard on a new idea. You might even have written a paper to explore it. You know that it's brilliant.

But no matter how worthwhile the idea or how clever and lucid the writing, it will just sit on your hard drive, gathering electronic dust, if you can't convince reviewers and editors that the work ought to be published.

Consider this note from the Writing Cooperative, a handy source of ideas for people who want to be read. Elise Welburn Martin shares, "If you don't capture their interest in the first 10–20 seconds, they are not going to engage in what could be the start of a beautiful relationship!"[1] Just think about that: ten to twenty seconds. (This is probably about half the time it took you to read this chapter to this point. Do you want to keep reading to find out how to solve this problem?)

Nearly everybody who is considering whether to publish something is inundated by ideas—both from people they know and so-called over-the-transom inquiries, which arrive every day. If you don't generate excitement about what you want to write, editors won't read what you have to say.

Every writer faces the challenge of hooking the people who are the gatekeepers that block writers from reaching a larger audience. As Martin puts it, "when writing creates curiosity in the reader, they are going to stay and continue to read."[2] You write effectively by understanding that you need to begin with a good pitch. The most important thing about writing those first few paragraphs is that you're framing the chance to excite your reader—and keep the reader reading. The following sections provide some proven ways of using that hook to convey interesting and important ideas that help to open that gate.

KNOW YOUR AUDIENCE, AND MAKE YOUR PITCH ACCORDINGLY

Editors and reviewers are supposed to be thinking about their audience every minute. You should do the same. If there's one key to a successful pitch, it's this: Make sure to read the publication for which you want to write so that you can pitch something they'll publish. And let them know that you know that.

There are four kinds of writing outlets that you might encounter. Each has a different audience—and a different kind of editor. Following a description of these four outlets, we'll provide ideas of the ways to approach the editors of each. In all cases, you need

Figure 8.1. Source: Getty Images, Creative #165722418; credit: Getty Images/XonkArts.

to have your pitchfork sharpened to win editorial interest and potentially bring your topic to a wider audience of readers.

First, there is the *academic journal*. The audience here may be professional colleagues, and it's become the central way in which researchers communicate with colleagues and burnish their academic reputations. Academics know the big issues in the field, how their ideas will resonate, and which journals are most likely to be the best fit. If you are working to sort this out, make sure to check with senior scholars in the field, who will be happy to help you here. To get published, however, you need to make sure that the editor—and the all-important reviewers—are intrigued with the first few paragraphs before they move on.

Second, *blogs* have become increasingly important and influential, especially in the world of public affairs. Many professionals and researchers turn to them to get a quick fix on important issues. Analysts have found that the ideal blog length shouldn't take more than seven minutes to read (or 1,600 words). Some publications look for posts that are half that length. If you're interested in submitting something to a blog, read other posts to get a sense of what readers are most likely to want to read. Determine not just the typical length but also the tone of the posts, whether they are written in the first person, whether they are casual or formal, whether they use hyperlinks, and so on. Armed with that information, tailor your pitch accordingly.

Third, there are *commentaries*. Well-read publications like *GovExec*, Route Fifty, *Governing*, and *Government Finance Review*, among others, have become increasingly influential in public debates. They strive to translate research into news you can use, especially for government practitioners. These publications have editors whose evaluation rests on their editorial focus, the quality of the argument, and on the skill with which the commentary is presented. They often have a large audience—but reaching that audience means first framing a pitch that excites the editor.

Fourth, there are *op-eds*, the more traditional short-form pieces of writing. The op-ed gets its name from the shorthand for "opposite the editorial page" from the days when everyone read opinions in the printed newspaper. These pieces tend to be high-reward, high-risk ventures, with wider readership but smaller odds of success. Editors at high-prestige newspapers like the *New York Times*, *Wall Street Journal*, and the *Washington Post* get deluged with a tsunami of submissions. Trish Hall, who used to be in charge of the *New York Times* op-ed page, shares, "I read many pieces, a number so high that I never counted it. There was no time."[3] That's because submissions sometimes can run into the hundreds, every day.

If you want to crack the editorial page, write smart and short. The typical op-ed can't be more than eight hundred words (see chapter 6 on how to write for length). You'll also need to know what kind of argument is most likely to tantalize the editor. The pieces most likely to be attractive are those that shine a light on something new or unexpected. Deep analysis of the news of the day isn't likely to be appealing.

Fifth, there are *books*. Book editors get many (sometimes hundreds) of pitches per week, and they often don't even have time to read them. Instead, they hand them over to an editorial assistant to consider what deserves to be passed on. A good pitch is essential to get an editor's—or an assistant's—attention.

Another bit of advice comes from a book agent, who suggests that "you will need to make a fan out of your acquisition editor."[4] Having a good friend in your editor is one of the most important ways of navigating the often long and convoluted book process.

Then, too, it's important to have patience. *Gone with the Wind*, for example, went on to win a Pulitzer Prize after being rejected by nearly forty publishers before one accepted it. Each of us has had book editors turn us down. We've also had proposals that ultimately proved successful but that took months to make it through the review process. We've even had book proposals that editors have never even responded to. The best way to get through the door is to begin by knowing the publisher's audience and how best to appeal to the people who read those books—and to remember that every bit of communication with the editor is one more way to create and strengthen the relationship with the person who will be making the decision about whether to publish your work.

FOR ACADEMIC JOURNALS, THE ABSTRACT IS FAR MORE IMPORTANT THAN YOU MIGHT THINK

It's an arduous process to produce an article for an academic journal. You labor mightily to polish your language and find the perfect source for every reference note. Finally, you're ready to celebrate submitting the paper to the journal for review. And then the journal wants you to write a 150-word abstract to go along with your paper. So, worn out, you dash something down, include it with your paper, and hit "Submit."

Most journal reviewers will say that they can smell those abstracts from a long distance away. A poorly written abstract can scuttle the odds for a paper even before the reviewer gets to the first page.

Many abstracts for professional journals are written in technical jargon that a reviewer—and later, a reader—cannot readily understand. Sometimes the abstract simply repeats the first few paragraphs of a paper, which is never useful. Sometimes the abstract is just sloppy.

It's important to remember that, in the academic world, the abstract occupies those critical ten to twenty seconds when you can capture interest. It should not be just a summary of findings. It's the pitch to editors and to reviewers. If you don't excite them, you reduce your chance of publication. Here are some tips for writing a good abstract:

- Sleep on it. The abstract shouldn't be the last thing you write, when you're exhausted after finishing a paper. Come back fresh, with new energy.
- Tell the reader the general problem you are addressing and why it matters.

- Lay out the theory that lies behind the work, and explain how you are moving the theory forward. But avoid the temptation to jump deeply into theoretical jargon that only insiders would understand.
- Explain (briefly and in plain English) what methodological approach you are using, even if you're writing a technical piece.
- Don't save the big finish for the end of the paper. Tell the reader what you've found. The reader is more likely to read what you've written if the end of the journey seems worth the effort.
- Consider adding an extra bit of polish, a sparkle that lures the reader (and reviewer), which should never be written when you've run out of gas.

EDITORS FOR GENERAL AUDIENCE PUBLICATIONS ARE ESPECIALLY LOOKING FOR A SHARP PITCH

Editors at blogs, commentaries, and subject-oriented publications are generally less interested in theory or methodology. They sometimes have greater flexibility about length but are often much more ruthless about the focus of the pieces they publish and work hard to cultivate a distinctive editorial vision.

Every column, article, or blog post has a particular audience. *RouteFifty*, for example, focuses on state and local government officials who are looking for fresh insights to help do their jobs better. Its parent company, *GovExec*, has an audience primarily of federal government officials, and its readers want thoughtful pieces on the issues surrounding the federal workforce and how-to guides for their personal finances within the federal benefits system. Governing.com has a similar audience as *RouteFifty*, but it tends to run more pieces each day. There also are many more similar publications in the broader policy world.

Your pitch shouldn't be long. Start with a powerful, evocative first sentence (written, if you can, in the style of the publication). Then, in lively and engaging sentences, add a couple of sentences about how you would develop your argument. Framing all of this in the context of your potential audience (although you don't have to do this explicitly) can strengthen the case.

Typically, it's better to test out an editor's interest in your idea, not to start out with a draft of a fully finished piece, which cuts the editor out of the process. An unsolicited blog, commentary, or article will be more likely to get a simple "yes" or "no" in response (and more likely a "no") rather than the desirable "Let's work on this." Enlisting an editor as a partner improves the writing—and the odds of publication.

OPTING FOR AN OP-ED

Hitting the op-ed page, especially of major newspapers, is notoriously difficult. Since many papers have syndicated columnists whose work they are contracted to run, the space available is limited. Moreover, editors tend to favor prominent authors and those with whom they have a long-standing relationship. For others, placing an op-ed is difficult—but not impossible.

Most newspapers have the contact information for their op-ed editors or their submission mailboxes available on their websites. That is the place to start. It can be tempting to look for back-door avenues for publication, but most newspapers insist that all submissions come in through their web portal. That makes it much easier to channel the tsunami.

What matters most is framing the right pitch. In preparing a draft, it's crucial to be hard-nosed in trimming the work to about eight hundred words. Some newspapers will only run even shorter pieces, perhaps seven hundred words or fewer, so it's crucial to be sharp and focused. It's a very rare op-ed editor who will ask you to make a piece *longer.* You'll almost always need to cut. It's best to do that before submission. That conveys a sense of professionalism—and it keeps the message more clearly in your own hands.

Faced with a huge number of submissions and a small amount of space, most op-ed editors will put a pitch aside if the first sentence or two doesn't hook them. It's crucially important, therefore, to craft these sentences carefully. No matter how interesting ideas might be, editors will never get to them if the beginning doesn't grab them.

HOW TO CATCH AN EDITOR'S ATTENTION FOR A BOOK IDEA

Turning a manuscript into a book is more difficult than it used to be because, quite simply, not as many people are reading books and not as many books are being published. There's less money in library budgets. Online resources have risen in importance. As a result, libraries in general—and academic libraries in particular—are buying fewer books. That, in turn, has changed the calculus for academic books because standing orders from libraries once kept many academic presses alive. These pressures have reduced the number of academic presses and have put economic pressure on all the presses that remain. Even textbook publishers have seen their markets shrink because of the widespread availability of used books and books for rent.

There are three basic kinds of book publishers: textbook publishers, which produce books for tailored markets, especially large undergraduate courses; academic presses, which produce scholarly books; and trade presses, which produce books for the broader market. Most academic writers aim for the middle piece of this sandwich because academic presses are more likely to be interested in their research and because the prestige of presses is important in faculty promotion decisions.

Editors of academic presses tend to be most interested in books on intriguing topics that advance theory and will attract readers. However, the line between academic presses and trade presses has started to blur. Some academic presses seek books that not only advance theory but also are likely to appeal to more general readers. Some trade presses are interested in finding ideas that create new intellectual capital.

The key to success with book editors is finding the press that has created a specialty in the topic you are writing about (what publishers call "the list")—and then getting the editor to read your manuscript. Reading an entire book-length manuscript, of course, would take a great deal of time, so publishers tend to prefer reviewing a short (ten pages or so) proposal first.

Here are the elements of a good book proposal:

- A good title and a lively table of contents, free of jargon, can often be the best way to get the editor's juices flowing.
- A description of the audience.
- Summary of the book's argument. Why should anyone read it?
- How the argument will be developed. This should be a discussion of the book's methods.
- Other books in the field. What other books are similar to yours?
- What's distinctive? What would be different about your book?
- A chapter outline. This ought to give a brief three-to-four sentence summary of each of the book's chapters.
- Length and delivery date. This would detail the book's length (in words) and when you would propose to submit the finished book to the publisher.
- What matters most of all is describing a book that would be worth reading in a way that the editor will want to be the book's first reader.

PLAY THE LONG GAME

Most journals require that you submit a paper exclusively to them. The same holds true for blogs, online publications, op-eds, and book proposals. Multiple submissions to different outlets tend to annoy editors, especially if they invest time and energy in the idea only to find the proposal submission has also gone to someone else. If you're caught doing this once, you don't need to go back to the estranged editor ever again.

Remember that the publishing world is a very small place. Editors know each other and often share thoughts behind the scenes. If a book doesn't fit one press's list, good editors will often suggest different presses you might try based on their personal relationships with other editors. You'll want to cultivate relationships with these editors for the long game.

All these ideas, in fact, point in the same direction: to move great ideas forward, sharpen your pitch and engage busy readers with ideas they will find truly exciting.

FROM OUR KEYBOARDS

In mid-2023 Kettl had an idea for a column for Governing.com. Here's the pitch he made to the editor:

> A tangential issue to state and local governments with huge implications for Medicaid and its costs. There's a huge shortage of some drugs, especially those used in treating cancers. Lots of complications in the cause of the issue. Turns out Medicaid is a huge market—maybe the largest market—for these drugs. States are being squeezed, and costs may well be driven up. So the states have a front seat on issues that intimately concern them and their residents, but they have no control over the process.
>
> Whaddya think?

And here was the editor's reply:

> Sounds promising. Guess I'd like a better idea of where you'd go with it—what your general takeaway would be.

Kettl wrote back:

> Here's the argument.

There's a crisis that's brewing for many cancer patients. The chemo drugs on which they depend are in very short supply and, in some cases, they're not available at all. For many physicians treating them, it's beyond the question of rationing the meds. Some patients just won't get anything, and in many cases there isn't a substitute.

The shortage is boiling over into other areas as well. The pandemic led to more diagnoses of ADHD, and more diagnoses led to more prescriptions for Adderall. That's now in super-short supply, and alternatives like Ritalin are now tough to get, too.

Medicaid is a major funder of these drugs. . . . There are some numbers around to discover how large a percentage of sales Medicaid funds. But it's a lot. And of course, like all Medicaid benefits, the costs are split between the feds and the states (and) all the states have outpatient drug coverage.

Kettl went on to explain that Medicaid is the largest and fastest-growing part of most states' budgets. While states can control some of their Medicaid policy positions, when it comes to drug coverage, they don't have control over who's paying how much for what. The states are on the hook financially, but the feds do the bargaining, and the drug companies have their own role in the game. Accountability for costs is muddled, and at the moment, the states are stuck.

The editor wrote back and gave the green light. A few weeks later, the column appeared.

NOTES

1. Elise Welburn Martin, "You Have 10–20 Seconds to Capture a Reader's Attention!," The Writing Cooperative, September 16, 2016, https://writingcooperative.com/you-have-10-20-seconds-to-capture-a-readers-attention-e58eeaf6cf69.

2. Martin, "You Have 10–20 Seconds."

3. "Former New York Times Editor on Writing to Get Someone's Attention—And Maybe Changing Their Mind," WBUR, published on

July 2, 2019, https://www.wbur.org/hereandnow/2019/07/02/trish-hall -writing-to-persuade-book.

4. Alexander Field, "The Anatomy of a Compelling Book Proposal," The Bindery, https://www.thebinderyagency.com/articles/the-anatomy -of-a-compelling-book-proposal (accessed November 1, 2023).

Chapter 9

Keep Your Friends Close

Find Partners in Your Effort to Be Understood

General—and then President—Ulysses S. Grant was determined to complete his memoir before throat cancer ended his life at sixty-three. He had a substantial amount of material, all written in his own hand, and he was ready to sign a contract with a publisher. But the famous author and humorist Mark Twain (see figure 9.1) heard about the deal and thought he could arrange something far better for Grant.[1]

Grant was reluctant to back out of the deal he had been negotiating with the first publisher. For him, it was a matter of honor, and he did not want to walk away from the discussions he had been having, even though Twain was convinced it was a very bad deal. The next day, Twain returned with what he promised to be a better offer: Twain would arrange for the book to be published through a subscription service with a strong press, one in which salespeople (often Civil War veterans) went door to door to make advance sales. Grant was convinced and took Twain's deal.

As Grant wrote, he shared the drafts with Twain, who offered advice on how to frame the argument and help in proofreading. Grant saw the book as a way to mark his accomplishments in life, and he seized on Twain's deal to provide financial support for his family when he was gone. Just days after he finished writing,

Figure 9.1. Mark Twain. Source: Wikimedia Commons: MarkTwain.LOC. jpg; credit: Wikimedia Commons.

in fact, the throat cancer took his life, but Twain's deal making proved an enduring legacy for Grant's family. A year after Grant died, the publisher sent his widow a check for $200,000, the biggest royalty check in history until that point. The book has been in print ever since. Interested readers can buy the Harvard University Press version, and it continues to rank high on Amazon's bestseller list.

It's hard to imagine that tremendous success without Grant's remarkable skill as a writer—and with Twain's help as agent and editor.

His name didn't hurt either. What better author on American politics could there be than someone whose name began "U. S."? (Even if the "S" became his middle initial because of a typographical error.)

FRIENDS CAN HELP ANY WRITER

Though writing itself may often be a solitary effort, there isn't a writer alive who can't benefit from bringing friends and colleagues into the process. There are at least three ways this can work.

They can help develop the argument. The first step for any writer is to figure out what to write about. Mulling over thoughts and doing online research are good starts. But tossing ideas around with a mentor or with colleagues can help find the holes in an idea or fire up enthusiasm to keep on going. It can be especially useful in determining whether anyone other than the author would be interested in the project to begin with.

Finding an idea is, of course, only the first step in the writing process. Narrowing it down is still harder. As dissertation advisers sometimes tell their PhD students, "It's best to write just one dissertation at a time, instead of trying to write about everything you care about." The same challenge faces any writer tackling anything from a short paper to a long book. A project needs a strong, unifying idea, and the best way to sharpen that idea is often to talk it through with friends—in part to get reactions and in part to listen to how it sounds when spoken out loud. (Remember the utility of talking to the dog, as we discussed in chapter 1. But long walks or swimming laps can work just as well.)

Beyond developing and refining ideas, entirely new ones can come up for people who filter their conversations in search of fodder. One of this book's authors was a junior faculty member at a dinner for a prospective university job candidate. It was a casual and friendly conversation, and to take some of the heat off the exhausted job candidate, a senior faculty member turned to the junior scholar. "Why don't you guys in public administration write about the most important administrative institution in the country?" he asked. "What's that?" the junior scholar replied, taking the bait. "The Federal Reserve," the senior scholar replied. The more the junior scholar thought about the question, the more he knew that the senior scholar was right. There was virtually nothing in the public administration literature about the Fed. So he launched the project, was able to publish it at a top university press, found the book very favorably reviewed in the *New York Times*, and used it as an important part of his case for tenure. Without that dinner conversation, the book never would have been written.

They can review the draft. No one gets writing right the first time. Good writing is the product of a process. Comments on a draft can make that process far better. As brilliant author and essayist Leo Rosten said, "If at first you don't succeed, before you try again, stop to figure out what you did wrong."[2] That's where friends, colleagues, and mentors can step in. They'll often spot the jargon that has become so familiar as to seem like plain English to the author. They'll say whether they get bored with the piece.

Perhaps the most important contribution another reader can make is to ask questions about sections that are confusing or explanations that seem to be missing. When those questions can't be answered, it may be a clue that the author needs to do some more research. In other instances, the writer may have assumed that everyone will have the same background, and that might not be the case.

They can help find a publisher. Whether you're trying to get an op-ed published or a column or a book, there can be a giant gap between you and the publication or the publisher. One option is to find an agent. There's been a great deal written about the best ways to procure a good agent, but one of the most promising is through an introduction by a friend.

Over forty years ago, one of this book's authors who wanted an agent worked at a magazine with a woman whose father was a well-known writer. He had a long-standing and successful relationship with a major agency and had connected his daughter to an agent there for her own work. The friend made an introduction, a deal with the agent was closed, and a year later, the book was published. But the story doesn't end there. Some years later, the agent was suggested by this book's author to a friend who wanted to write a children's book. Yet another introduction was made to the same agent, and the book called *Anthony the Perfect Monster* was the result.[3] (Note: this agent negotiated the contract for the book you're reading now.)

No less a luminary than Mark Twain needed help in getting published for the first time for his short story, "The Celebrated Jumping Frog of Calaveras County." He was rejected by the publisher G. W. Carlton (which, appropriately, went out of business in 1916). Fortuitously, a Californian friend of his, Charles H. Webb, told Twain that he would publish the book himself, and the book did so well that a different publisher offered to put into print his adventures on a trip to Europe and the Holy Land called *The Innocents Abroad.*

Everyone needs help in finding the best place for a piece of writing, and that is never truer than at the beginning of a career. The problem frequently is the same as that with borrowing money. Banks are inclined to lend you money only if you don't really need it. Similarly, newspaper, magazine, and book publishers are most inclined to work with someone who has already successfully written for newspapers, magazines, or publishing houses.

A friend or mentor can be invaluable in making an original introduction and vouching for the writer's proposal. Sometimes a friend may be particularly helpful in identifying the best outlet for a paper. This is especially important for younger scholars who need to assemble a publication record for tenure.

AI: FRIEND OR FOE?

Improvements in technology have long come hand in hand with distributing writing more broadly. In the fifteenth century, Johannes Gutenberg developed a printing process using movable type, which made it vastly easier to share writing with a far larger collection of readers. Centuries of printing advancement followed until the internet (for better or worse) made anyone with a cell phone a potential publisher who could reach thousands or millions of readers.

This sequence of forces has fundamentally democratized writing. And now the rise of artificial intelligence in the 2020s has brought yet another revolution. Not only could technology help authors get their words down on paper, it could suggest which words, sentences, and paragraphs ought to be written.

So, then, is AI your friend or foe? It depends. For professional writers, it certainly poses a threat. Hollywood's Writers Guild went on strike in 2023, in part to get a contract that would limit the degree to which studios could use AI (see figure 9.2) to write scripts.

"History has shown that, when technology has replaced humans, we've created new purposes for ourselves," shares the *Guardian*. "But in its eternal quest for self-improvement, is there a danger that AI will continually outpace us by making us redundant more quickly than we can redefine our roles?"[4] Futurists have made bold predictions about how AI will change the jobs of virtually everyone.

But this book wasn't written for people who make their living by writing but rather those who simply want to be better at that skill and, in so doing, give their ideas an opportunity to flourish for an audience that can use them to make the world a better place.

And for you, AI is likely to be an invaluable tool for quickly pulling together information from across the internet. It can suggest ideas that might not have occurred to you, arguments that others have used, and emerging issues in your field. Of course, at least for now, it has no conscience and no soul, so it can produce

Figure 9.2. Source: Getty Images, Creative #1450370018; credit: Getty Images/KATERYNA KON/SCIENCE PHOTO LIBRARY.

ideas without ethics or feeling. And it often lacks the distinctly human touch that comes from engaging writing.

It's no secret that writers and editors—as well as students and professors—are in an arms race to discover new uses for AI and to prevent its unscrupulous use. That's been going on with a variety of technologies since the dawn of written words thousands of years ago, but the tension has accelerated with the explosion of new tools for writing.

If there's any prediction that emerges from the decades— indeed, the millennia—of technology in writing, it's that AI's critics can't sweep its opportunities under writers' rugs. New communications technologies, once invented, aren't turned off. It will take a decade or more to understand just what AI does well, what it can't, and what it might do well in the future.

Some commentators have suggested that AI could help writers in many new ways: as one *Wall Street Journal* columnist offers,

"[AI] gives me something I can revise and work from, instead of starting from a blank page."[5]

Other uses include the following:

AI can generate a first draft of ideas from which writers can revise. That, of course, is a slippery slope. It can be tempting to slide from "This is just a first draft" to "The AI draft is substantially the one I'll turn in."

AI can generate titles. For authors who aren't sure how to title their work, AI can provide fresh suggestions.

AI can help you edit your work down. It's always easier to write long and then cut to length (see chapter 6). AI is getting better at suggesting how to do this.

AI can change the tone of your writing. If your writing is too stiff, AI can suggest ways of softening the edges. It can even assess the tone of your writing to see if it's the target you want to hit.

AI will certainly create advances that we haven't even thought of yet. That will surely open new opportunities in writing, just as the invention of the printing press made it possible to share ideas on a scale never before possible and the rise of the internet created instantaneous communication of ideas. AI is likely to stir innovations of just this scale—or larger.

FROM OUR KEYBOARDS

Here's a case study on the importance of keeping your friends close.

One of the authors suffered the same fate as Mark Twain: the first effort at publishing a book was rejected by the publisher. But the author developed a good relationship with the editor, especially at professional meetings. When it came time for the next book, the author had far better luck. Because of that relationship, the book moved swiftly off the editor's desk. (In fact, a big secret of the publishing business is that the process can move at lightning speed or can drag on for years. The difference lies in the editor's enthusiasm for the book.) The process went smoothly into the hands of reviewers and, from there, into publication. That led to another book with the press and then another.

It's good to cultivate friends and to keep them for a long time.

NOTES

1. "How Mark Twain Helped Ulysses S. Grant Write His Personal Memoirs," National Park Service, https://www.nps.gov/articles/000/how-mark-twain-helped-ulysses-s-grant-write-his-personal-memoirs.htm (accessed November 1, 2023).

2. "Leo Rosten Quotes," AZ Quotes, https://www.azquotes.com/author/12676-Leo_Rosten (accessed November 1, 2023).

3. Angelo Decesare, *Anthony the Perfect Monster* (New York: Random House Books for Young Readers, 1996).

4. Henry Williams, "I'm a Copywriter. I'm Pretty Sure Artificial Intelligence Is Going to Take My Job," *Guardian*, January 24, 2023, https://www.theguardian.com/commentisfree/2023/jan/24/chatgpt-artificial-intelligence-jobs-economy.

5. Alexandra Samuel, "Do You Hate to Write? These Tech Tools May Help," *Wall Street Journal*, May 13, 2023, https://www.wsj.com/articles/writing-tech-tools-help-cd762aec.

Chapter 10

The Care and Feeding of Editors

How to Make the Writing Experience a Collaboration

Editors and reviewers are the essential conduits to translate an author's ideas into a forum that everyone else can read. The good ones can make you happier with your work by helping you imagine directions you hadn't thought of.

For one of the authors of this book, it was a privilege to be edited by Jim Michaels, the longtime editor of *Forbes* magazine, during a period when it was clearly one of the three most reliable and respectable publications in the world of business, alongside *BusinessWeek* and *Fortune*. Nothing that went into his typewriter (and later his computer) came out untouched. And everything came out better. (There's an irony here in that Michaels insisted that no sentence should begin with the word "and," a stylistic belief that has since fallen by the wayside nearly everyplace.)

Michaels, like many of the best editors, could be described as irascible, a word that is often connected with the word editor just as fires are often described as raging and it's common to hear that inflation is crippling. Other excellent editors are somewhat easier to get along with. William Shawn, the editor of the *New Yorker* for thirty-five years, was described in his obituary as "quiet, considerate, infinitely courteous."[1]

Whatever their temperament, there's one important truth about editors and reviewers: They must be treated with respect no matter what you think of their skill. You may not believe that you should have to put money in a parking meter, but if you don't, your car may be towed away. Editors are a lot like that.

WHY IS IT IMPORTANT TO WORK WELL WITH EDITORS?

This question may seem obvious, but based on these authors' experiences of editing others, many writers don't seem to know the answer.

For one thing, if you can turn the relationship with your editor from a hierarchical interaction into a collaborative one, it's likely that the experience will be more pleasant and the final product will be better. Here is one tip: When you feel like editors have improved your work, let them know. Few writers do this, and only the vainest editor won't appreciate it. And there's a distinct possibility that the editor's ideas—and even comments from reviewers—will actually strengthen the work. It's important to remember that editors don't exist to torpedo your writing. After all, editors get excited by—and are paid for—the opportunity to find and publish great work. They get no satisfaction from sending rejections. You can help them succeed by allowing them to help you succeed.

What's more, there's every chance that you may want to work with the same editor again in the future. If you've been a frustrating writer who is whiny and difficult, attached to every participle and comma, that opportunity diminishes. For the most prestigious publications, it's a buyers' market, with many proposals coming in for each that's accepted. Establishing good relationships will leave the door open for further submissions. A strong relationship can keep the door open wide.

Additionally, there's always the possibility that you can learn something valuable. Editors are frequently experts in the topic about which you're writing and may have a historical sense that you lack. Writers who pay attention to their comments (see figure 10.1), questions, and changes accumulate important information that can be of use in the future. Each of us can look back on work with editors that taught important lessons, which, in turn, have paid off for decades.

Figure 10.1. Editorial Comments. Source: Getty Images, Creative #1183393265; credit: Getty Images/filo.

SEVEN TIPS FOR KEEPING EDITORS HAPPY

As we wrote in chapter 8, *read the publication* before you write for it. All outlets for writing are different from one another in important ways. A one-size-fits-all approach is far less likely to fit the style and tone of the publication or satisfy the editor with whom you're working.

Meet your deadlines. Although this is a concept frequently ignored in academia, editors will invariably be much happier if promised work comes in on time. It helps them to plan their own calendars as well as the schedule for their publication. What if you just can't meet a deadline? Then let the editor know right away, and ask for an extension. If that's not possible, then do whatever you have to do to get your work in on time.

Pick your battles. When an editor renders something inaccurate, which can happen, it's perfectly reasonable to point that out before your words are seen by others. After all, it's your reputation that's at stake. But for matters of word choice or questions of punctuation, it's wise to swallow pride and let editorial decisions stand. Writers who insist on getting their way risk hurting the relationship and that can come back to haunt them.

Listen. Often when you've proposed an idea, editors will give you guidance about the kind of information they want included in the work. It's possible that their counsel is different than what you had in mind, but if you disagree, this is the time to have a discussion. Don't just ignore them and risk their potential frustration later.

Ask questions. If you're not clear about what the editor wants— and some recommendations can certainly be unclear—get them to refine their thoughts before you stay up all night writing, only to discover that you've written something they can't use.

Stay in touch. If, as you start to build your piece, you discover that you're confused about the blueprint, there's no shame in consulting your editor for clarification. This can save a lot of time revising later.

Figure 10.2.   Editor at Work. Source: Getty Images, Creative #172257057;
credit: Getty Images/biffspandex.

Be prepared to revise whatever you do. Editors and reviewers are entitled to ask for changes to submissions. They often do. As painful as it may be, comply as cheerfully as possible and make the changes they request, while still striving to preserve the integrity of the piece. If asked to make a change that will force an inaccuracy into your prose, then discuss the issue, but keep it civil, and be entirely clear about the nature of your objection. Even if you disagree with the editors'—or reviewers'—suggestions, it's important to respond thoughtfully to each comment. Remember that every conversation with an editor is laying the foundation for another project you might want to do in the future.

Don't be shocked when you confront reviewer number two. Some peer reviewers prefer to be snarky instead of helpful; are committed to their own ideologies and beliefs regardless of the power of your research; and treat authors as slightly less than human. What are you to do when you confront one? Courtney Berger, executive editor at Duke University Press, gives some good advice: "Go ahead and vent—but be careful about where and how you do so."[2] Among her other solid suggestions are the following: clarify your vision; talk to your editor; know when to cut your losses; and "make your response about you, not the reviewer."[3]

A GUIDE TO STYLE GUIDES

Many publications have their own formal style guides, which are provided to ensure that there's a standard approach to grammar, punctuation, tone, wording, and best practices for writing.

Before submitting a manuscript of any kind, it's wise to ask what style guide the publication uses, or whether it has one of its own. For example, Rowman & Littlefield, the publisher of this book, uses one of the most popular guides, the *Chicago Manual of Style*. The *Chicago Manual* is commonly the choice in book publishing both for fiction and nonfiction as well as for academic papers in the arts and humanities. The *Associated Press Stylebook* is common for newspapers and magazines. And the Modern Language Association's *MLA Handbook* is often used for academic writing and is required by many journal publishers.

When following a style guide, it's important to be clear about which edition your editor wants. For example, the seventeenth edition of the *Chicago Manual* differs from the sixteenth in a variety of important ways, such as this: "A comma no longer follows etc. at the end of a list unless required by the surrounding syntax."[4]

Individual publications may not wait for a style book to catch up with the sentiments of their editors and will make internal decisions to change the way their writers write. These decisions aren't made on a whim but are generally carefully thought through. For example, on July 20, 2020, the *Washington Post* published the following:

> Beginning immediately, the *Washington Post* will uppercase the B in Black to identify the many groups that make up the African diaspora in America and elsewhere. This decision comes after extensive discussions with members of our own news organization, consultations with editors in other newsrooms nationwide and evaluations of commentary and analyses by numerous thought leaders and organizations of influence in the Black community.[5]

The change in the *Post*'s style was part of the broader debate we saw in chapter 1.

All stylistic preferences aren't necessarily codified in writing, but they are important to know for writers who want to avoid frustrating their editors. Richard Eisenberg, a longtime writer and editor about aging issues, points out that the often-used "silver tsunami" seems to suggest that "older adults are a natural disaster." Phrases like "elderly" and "senior citizens" raise similar problems. The *AP Stylebook,* he says, contends that it is much better to use more-specific terms, like "people 65 and over," or perhaps "an exercise program for women over 70."[6]

FROM OUR KEYBOARDS

Some years ago, all three of the authors of this book were involved in the Government Performance Project, an effort published in *Governing* magazine and funded by the Pew Charitable Trusts. One of its goals was to evaluate the management capacity of the states.

On one occasion the evaluation of Virginia was exceedingly positive. The joint efforts of academics (led by Kettl) and the journalists (led by Barrett and Greene) led them to believe that Virginia should be given an A. But *Governing*'s editor at the time, Alan Ehrenhalt, was dubious about that accolade. Without going into the reasons behind his logic, based on his in-depth knowledge of the situation in that state, the grade was changed to an A–. He was persuasive. The change was made. And subsequently, the chief financial officer of the state acknowledged that the researchers involved had been somewhat oversold on the merits of the state in making their original judgment.

NOTES

1. Eric Pace, "William Shawn, 85, Is Dead; New Yorker's Gentle Despot," *New York Times*, December 9, 1992, https://www.nytimes.com/1992/12/09/obituaries/william-shawn-85-is-dead-new-yorker-s-gentle-despot.html.

2. "What to Do About Reviewer #2: Advice for Handling a Difficult Peer Review," *Duke University Press* (blog), https://dukeupress.wordpress.com/2019/09/16/what-to-do-about-reviewer-2-advice-for-handling-a-difficult-peer-review (accessed November 1, 2023).

3. "What to Do About Reviewer #2," *Duke University Press* (blog).

4. "What's New in the 17th Edition," *The Chicago Manual of Style Online*, https://www.chicagomanualofstyle.org/dam/jcr:3259cf8e-7d5f-4953-a660-6155ac88f4f1/What%27s%20New%20in%20CMOS17.pdf (accessed November 1, 2023).

5. "The *Washington Post* Announces Writing Style Changes for Racial and Ethnic Identifiers," *WashPost PR* (blog), July 29, 2020, https://www.washingtonpost.com/pr/2020/07/29/

washington-post-announces-writing-style-changes-racial-ethnic-identifiers.

6. Richard Eisenberg, "Ageism in the Media: An Insider's Perspective," *Generations,* September 20, 2023, https://generations.asaging.org/ageism-media-insiders-perspective.

Chapter 11

Downloading Some Facts about Social Media

The Evolving World of Online Communication Can Help You Accomplish Your Goals

Around 3500 BCE, somewhere near the Persian Gulf, some clever Sumerians created the earliest known written language in the form of pictographs. About 1,700 years later, a Sumerian epic poem has preserved the legend of that world-changing event, putting it into a perspective that even modern readers can understand: "Because the messenger, whose mouth was tired, was not able to repeat it, the lord of Kulaba patted some clay and wrote the message as if on a tablet."[1]

That was the beginning of written words. As the ages passed, their development progressed through the Egyptian culture, which found that people could write on papyrus and roll the writing into scrolls. Subsequently, Romans invented the codex, and scribes copied out entire volumes onto individual sheets of paper, which were bound and even sometimes paginated. And then—ta-da—Gutenberg invented the printing press, which fueled modern civilization's desire to communicate thoughts widely.

And now we complain because our emails don't go from here to there in under two seconds—or even that some people use email, when social media apps are faster.

The point of this brief history lesson is that writing has been an ever-evolving form, and the way it works at any point in time won't be the way it works in the future. At the core of the story, however, is this: for at least the last 5,500 years or so, humans have sought new ways to communicate ideas with each other through words. Writing, in fact, is one of the most enduring parts of human society. It's always been a matter of finding new technologies for doing that more successfully.

The most recent advance of any great magnitude for disseminating information to a broad audience has been the ever-evolving world of social media—the first time in history that people around the globe could communicate their ideas to hundreds, thousands, or millions of others and do so instantly (see figure 11.1).

Consider this: In 2020 about 24 million copies of daily American newspapers circulated in both online and print editions.[2] Let's compare that to United States newspaper circulation

Figure 11.1.   Source: Getty Images, Creative #150415588; credit: Getty Images/Dimitri Otis.

of 62 million in 1970, which was almost three times higher than fifty years later.[3]

And what is the comparison to social media?

As of August 2022, Barack Obama had 132 million followers on his Twitter (now X) account.[4] In January 2023 Donald Trump had about 150 million across a variety of platforms.[5] (And who had the largest number of Instagram followers? It was soccer great Cristiano Ronaldo, with 599 million.[6] That's ahead of any of the Kardashians.) Clearly, few followers are reading each and every one of the messages from either of the presidents, but then an awful lot of newspapers go unread every day too.

MAKING THE MOST OUT OF SOCIAL MEDIA

People who are trying to use social media to advance their goals of writing for impact are clearly chasing the future in a car with no headlights, driving down a curving road on a starless night. No one can really predict which platform will be the most popular or have the greatest influence on the audience a writer is trying to reach. One lesson emerges from recent years: social media isn't going away, and however you choose to access it, there can be significant benefits. While the platforms will inevitably change, here are six practices that we've found useful in the current world of social media that should continue to work well over time.

Use social media to market and promote your writing. The three authors of this book have cultivated significant followings on a variety of social media outlets as a way of attracting attention to individual pieces, pleasing click-hungry publishers, and attracting a larger audience.

Supplement posts about your own products with hyperlinks and references that will interest your followers. It's important to note that using social media just to market yourself dilutes its power. People are far more inclined to pay attention to what you have to say if you've established a reputation as a credible source of interesting information, not just as someone engaged in self-promotion.

Seek quality in followers, not quantity. Build your social media following with people who are likely to want to follow your topics. On most popular social media sites today, it's easy to gather up thousands of followers who want to sell you real estate or insurance or a passel of cash that you've implausibly inherited from a crown prince in a foreign land. That does you no good in your professional life, and it will only benefit those whose sense of ego is sufficiently fragile as to equate sheer numbers of followers with those who have value.

Follow sources in your field that you'd like to follow you. This not only can help to extend the reach of your posts, but it's an excellent way to keep up with news that may influence what you write. What's more, when doing your research, the individuals or organizations you're following can be a valuable shortcut to see what other people are writing about similar topics. In the old days, magazine writers turned to the *Readers' Guide to Periodical Literatur*e as a key resource to see what had been written about any given topic. This reference work still exists and certainly has its utility, but it is now only one of scores of ways to accomplish the same goal, with some form of social media providing it in a cheap, instantaneous fashion.

Check out what's trending. Social media is a good way to make sure your work is timely. The world changes with lightning speed, accelerating the aging process of a draft that was written just a week before. Social media highlights the ideas that are gathering steam most quickly. If you're looking for timely references to spark that important first paragraph in a piece, good hints can be found by looking at what's currently trending, as well as at the words or phrases—often labeled as hashtags on current social media sites—that draw the most reader interest.

Discover new research and potential contacts. Search engines that are available on a variety of social media platforms can help you find valuable sources. While established authorities on a particular topic are easily located through more traditional means, social media can surface new academic papers, journalistic articles, or significant news events, particularly those that have generated attention largely in local outlets.

Searches also can provide the news that a new report has just come out on a similar topic or about when a piece of expected upcoming legislation has just been unexpectedly quashed.

As with everything on social media (or, for that matter, everything that appears in writing anywhere), information needs to be double-checked for accuracy and potential bias.

There's no guessing where this will go. But two things are certain. One is that the pace of technology-supported writing will advance even more quickly in the future. The other is that the core job of translating one's own research, thoughts, feelings, and values into a form that can be shared with others will remain at the core of the process, no matter what.

NOTES

1. "Electronic Text Corpus of Sumerian Literature, Enmerkar and the Lord of Aratta: Translation, 500–514," Navigation Help, https://etcsl .orinst.ox.ac.uk/section1/tr1823.htm (accessed November 1, 2023).

2. Pew Research Center, Newspapers Fact Sheet, June 29, 2021, https: //www.pewresearch.org/journalism/fact-sheet/newspapers.

3. Statista Research Department, "Daily Newspaper Circulation in the U.S. and Soviet Union in Select Years between 1970 and 1989," Statista, published August 1, 1991, https://www.statista.com/statistics/1249604/ daily-newspaper-circulation-us-ussr-cold-war/.

4. "Twitter's Bot Problem: How Bad Is It for Businesses?" Spider AF, updated July 13, 2023, https://spideraf.com/media/articles/twitter-bot -problem-how-bad-is-it-for-businesses.

5. Statista Research Department, "Number of Followers of Donald Trump on Select Social Media Platforms as of January 2023," Statista, published January 2023, https://www.statista.com/statistics/1336497/ donald-trump-number-of-followers-selected-social-platforms.

6. "The 10 Most Followed Instagram Accounts in the World in 2023," *Forbes India*, August 16, 2023, https://www.forbesindia.com/article/ explainers/most-followed-instagram-accounts-world/85649/1.

Chapter 12

This Is the Chapter before the Conclusion . . . It's about Conclusions

Setting the Stage for Your Next Effort

As the prolific American songwriter and musician Bobby Womack, a 2009 inductee into the Rock and Roll Hall of Fame, said, "Leave them wanting more and you know they'll call you back."[1] His advice holds true for writing as well. There are many ways to accomplish this, which we've covered in prior chapters, but one of the most important is to have a good conclusion to your piece that makes readers curious to hear what more you may have to tell them in the future.

TRAPS TO AVOID

It can be tempting to use the last part of a writing project to launch a grand summary of all the ideas you've developed during the piece. Readers, however, will already have digested those points, and they won't pay much attention if they see a rehash of what has gone before.

Then there's the syndrome of "Now I've finally figured out what I wanted to say!" Many papers meander along, adding fact to fact and thought to thought. By the time it comes to wind up, the author has finally figured out what the piece is really all about and uses that as the conclusion. This is a perverse approach because it gives the conclusion a job the introduction should have accomplished. This often happens when a writer is under deadline/time pressure, throws the words down on paper, and hands it in without revisions.

Even worse, some conclusions have a lot of words but don't say anything. Consider, for example, whether the following conclusion for a term paper adds anything at all:

> In the process of undertaking this comprehensive research project, I have examined a multitude of sources, conducted extensive analyses, and delved deep into the subject matter. It is apparent that the findings and data collected throughout this investigation have shed light on various aspects of the topic, thus providing a substantial body of evidence to support the claims made in this study. Consequently, it can be reasonably surmised that the results obtained have significant implications and can potentially contribute to a broader understanding of the subject matter at hand.

The above, by the way, was written by an AI app, thus demonstrating that, for the moment at least, artificial intelligence doesn't necessarily have the intelligence to write great prose.

Then there's the "Sherlock Holmes" conclusion, which the University of North Carolina at Chapel Hill's Writing Center urges writers to avoid.[2] The supersleuth was famous for weaving together all the clues at the end of his investigations and surprising his audience with the solution to a crime. That might work in the hands of the famous fiction writer Arthur Conan Doyle—but it's a dangerous style for nonfiction writers. A conclusion that surprises readers is a conclusion that doesn't grow logically and organically from the argument that precedes it.

It's also wise to avoid conclusions that deflate readers, like several paragraphs that call for further research on the issue. When a writer focuses the reader on what a piece *doesn't say*, it detracts from what it *does*—and it leads the reader to ask why, if the unexplored issue is so interesting, the writer didn't examine it in the piece. There is always a long agenda of interesting puzzles that an author can explore in the next project. Tackling one problem at a time and writing about it well is the author's strongest strategy.

In conclusion, avoid starting your conclusion with the words "in conclusion." It's a lazy way to finish up a piece and doesn't add anything at all to it—just like the sentence that precedes this one.

WHAT THE FOUNDING FATHERS CAN TEACH US ABOUT CONCLUSIONS

The introduction and conclusion of a writing project ought to be like bookends, making everything in between stand up straight and tall.

More than one reader streamlines their work by reading just the introduction and conclusion and skimming all the rest. That, of course, never does justice to the subtleties of any author's hard work, but it does provide evidence that those two metaphorical bookends can sometimes be more important than what's in between.

There's often far more attention given to the introduction than to the conclusion. No surprise there. Often the conclusion is little more than an afterthought, tagged on at the end of a piece of writing once everything important has already been written. What's more, who doesn't have more energy about a project at its beginning than hours, days, weeks, or months later, when the project is at its end and there's pressure to get the darn thing in?

Following are three of the most powerful conclusions you'll ever find, written by some of the most elegant wordsmiths in American history. They all make that which preceded them more powerful and lead readers (or listeners) to want to hear more from their writers.

Figure 12.1. Benjamin Franklin, John Adams, and Thomas Jefferson Working on the Declaration of Independence. Source: Getty Images, Creative #158653366; credit: Getty Images/John Parrot, Stocktrek Images.

In the Declaration of Independence, Thomas Jefferson writes, "With a firm reliance on the protection of divine Providence, we mutually pledge to each other our Lives, our Fortunes and our sacred Honor."[3]

In Abraham Lincoln's Gettysburg Address, he concludes,

> [It is] for us to be here dedicated to the great task remaining before us—that from these honored dead we take increased devotion to that cause for which they gave the last full measure of devotion—that we here highly resolve that these dead shall not have died in vain—that this nation, under God, shall have a new birth of freedom—and that government of the people, by the people, for the people, shall not perish from the earth.[4]

From George Washington's Farewell Address (which was actually composed by Alexander Hamilton, who was a far better writer than Washington), we have the following: "I anticipate with pleasing expectation that retreat in which I promise myself to realize, without alloy, the sweet enjoyment of partaking, in the midst of my fellow-citizens, the benign influence of good laws under a free government, the ever-favorite object of my heart, and the happy reward, as I trust, of our mutual cares, labors, and dangers."[5]

These words have stood the test of time because they end with a punch that listeners or readers can't forget.

TIPS TO FOLLOW

Hark back to where you started. As one Broadway critic notes, "Many musicals end with the story looping back to its opening, presented to us once again with two hours of context and wisdom giving the same scenario a new and more complex shading."[6] While this is a powerful way to end a piece of writing, consider one cautionary note: don't just repeat the introduction. Make sure the conclusion does just as the critic suggests, which is to add a "new and more complex shading."

Synthesize the work's findings. It's not a good idea to recapitulate an article, blog, or book in its conclusion. After all, it's called a conclusion, not a summary. However, think of the conclusion as the opportunity to provide takeaways from the sum of the piece. (This is particularly useful for readers, as mentioned above, who only read the introduction and the conclusion.)

Ask, "So what?" Imagine that your reader is busy and wants to know what you think the reader ought to know before moving on. The reader has gotten this far in your piece, but telling your reader why the preceding was worth reading will help to make them hold your words in higher esteem.

Share implications. Telling your reader what impact your work might have for the theories in the field or, perhaps, for public policy can help answer the "So what?" question.

Place your work in a larger context. It's important not to overreach, but helping readers see the broader implications of your work can give it extra impact.

Consider, where possible, using a quote. When someone else says something more powerfully than you might be able to, quoting them at the conclusion can get you off the hook.

Keep it simple. Short, declarative language is powerful for the entirety of a piece of writing but is even more so in the end, when many readers won't have the patience to sludge their way through convoluted prose.

When you're done—end it! Rambling on and on and on in search of an appropriate conclusion is the surest way to make sure that nobody will finish reading what you've had to say.

FROM OUR KEYBOARDS

From the conclusion of *Bridgebuilders: How Government Can Transcend Boundaries to Solve Big Problems*, by William D. Eggers and Donald F. Kettl:

> We face some tough steps: building capacity to master the ten principles, weaving them together in a concerted whole, taking them

to scale, and building trust in our institution to support them as a strategy for twenty-first-century governance. That's not an easy road. But it's far better than the alternative of a government with performance and trust racing each other downhill, and it offers a different better road forward for the decades to come.

It offers the best opportunities for improving government's results and trust in public institutions. And that, in turn, provides the best foundations for strengthening democratic governance in the twenty-first century.[7]

NOTES

1. "Bobby Womack: The Last Soul Man," *Independent*, June 6, 2004, https://www.independent.co.uk/arts-entertainment/music/features/bobby-womack-the-last-soul-man-731289.html.

2. "Conclusions," The Writing Center, University of North Carolina at Chapel Hill, https://writingcenter.unc.edu/tips-and-tools/conclusions (accessed November 1, 2023).

3. Declaration of Independence (National Archives), https://www.archives.gov/founding-docs/declaration-transcript (accessed November 2, 2023).

4. Gettysburg Address (Library of Congress), https://www.loc.gov/resource/rbpe.24404500/?st=text (accessed November 2, 2023).

5. George Washington's Farewell Address (National Constitution Center), https://constitutioncenter.org/the-constitution/historic-document-library/detail/george-washington-farewell-address-1796 (accessed November 2, 2023).

6. Rebecca Alter, "There Are Only Two Types of Musical Endings That Matter," *Vulture* (*New York*), February 25, 2021, https://www.vulture.com/2021/02/there-are-only-two-types-of-musical-endings-that-matter.html.

7. William D. Eggers and Donald F. Kettl, *Bridgebuilders: How Government Can Transcend Boundaries to Solve Big Problems* (Boston: Harvard Business Press, 2023).

Conclusion

Daniel J. Boorstin, a historian and former librarian of Congress who managed the largest library in the world, had a special take on writing for impact. "I write to discover what I think," he says; then he adds, "After all, the bars aren't open that early."[1]

Boorstin has pointed to the most important lesson of this book: writing is about thinking and communicating those thoughts to readers. It's an intensely intimate relationship between the writer's mind and paper or screen. At the same time, it's supremely social because writers want to connect those thoughts to readers.

There are three different ways to do that. First, writers can put the words down as they occur to them. That's quick and seems to be the approach taken by many who write exclusively on social media. But that won't pass scrutiny by any editor. It may work for some writing savants, but it's generally not effective for most of us mortals. Stream-of-consciousness writing depends on the rare facility to think about something with a clear beginning, middle, and end buried in your mind, with you waiting only for a writing tool, whether pencil, pen, or keyboard, to dig it up and share it. Absent that extremely rare ability, most writers need to rearrange paragraphs and sentences and find better words before calling it quits.

Alternatively, writers can work through their ideas in their heads, turning them over and examining them from different perspectives, sharpening them, refining them, and rethinking them, before putting a word to paper or screen. That's an elegant approach, and it may work well for some, but it's a luxury denied to anyone who faces a deadline.

Then there's a middle ground. Writers can lay down sentences and paragraphs as they come to mind and then go back and move them around, revising and revising again until the thoughts flow smoothly, the words are pristine, and the flow of logic is clear. For some, it's useful to have an outline to guide the writing—and this can be crucial for particularly long pieces, like a book. But sticking stubbornly to the preconceived notion in an outline can limit the lovely capacity to discover rich new ideas as the words flow out.

We lean toward the middle-ground approach (mainly because it's what works for all of us). We begin with ideas—sometimes big ones, sometimes not. We research until there's no more time for research or until we really think we have concluded that we know what we need to write. Or we find ourselves circling back to the same ideas, which suggests there's no point in trudging on. Then the writing begins. We may not immediately be sure of the best way to begin, but we generally know where we want to go.

We write for many reasons. We love words. We sometimes get paid. In a way akin to acting, we enjoy parading our work before others. We hope to make the world a better place, and this is one way we want to do that. And we relish the process of discovery that writing provides. As American novelist and short story writer Flannery O'Connor explained in better words than ours, "I write to discover what I know."[2]

Assuming that you're not reading this conclusion before you read any other chapters (like a friend of ours who jumps to the end of a scary story to make sure everything turns out all right), we hope that you'll now find that your writing has more impact than it did before you started. If we've been successful, then the journey will have been worthwhile for all of us.

Before we leave you, we'd like to sign off with a lovely sentiment about writing and life from American poet Sylvia Plath. Says she, "Let me live, love, and say it in good sentences."[3]

NOTES

1. "Memorable Quotes on Writing & Editing," Pen4rent.com, https://pen4rent.com/resources/memorable-quotes-on-writing (accessed November 2, 2023).

2. "Flannery O'Connor Quotes," Goodreads.com, https://www.goodreads.com/quotes/150203-i-write-to-discover-what-i-know (accessed November 2, 2023).

3. Goodreads, https://www.goodreads.com/quotes/7224372-god-let-me-think-clearly-and-brightly-let-me-live (accessed November 2, 2023).

Acknowledgments

This book builds on the foundation of our work with a broad collection of people who are especially adept at the art of writing for impact in public policy. They've been instrumental in helping us to develop the ideas that are contained in this book, and we're very grateful to them: David Ammons, John Bartle, Kristin Clark, Alan Ehrenhalt, Richard Eisenberg, Steve Fehr, William Glasgall, Alisha Gillis, Phil Joyce, John Martin, Don Moynihan, Michael Pagano, Josie Schaffer, Chrisopher Swope, and Gary Van Landingham.

Beyond that, it would be unfair and unreasonable not to give due credit to the many people who have worked with us, talked endlessly with us about good writing, and guided us in learning more about writing and researching than we could have achieved through any means except for reading (sadly, some of the following are no longer with us): Ben Baldwin, Herbert Barrett, Phyllis Berman, Paul Blustein, Myrna Blyth, Charles Bowen, Pamela Bowen, Caroline Cournoyer, Elizabeth Daigneau, Margaret Degnan, Jimmie Denley, Jean Dimeo, Ray Evans, James Fesler, Jack Fuller, Mark Geiger, BeBe Greene, Jefferson Grigsby, Don Hatfield, Anne Jordan, Penny Lemov, Charles Lindblom, Sylvia Liroff, Bill Lucia, Melissa Maynard, Angus McEachran; John McMillan, James Michaels, Zach Patton, Lisa Ruddick, Howard Rudnitsky, Dero Saunders, Tom Shoop, Geoff Smith, Ed Stannard, Paul Sturm, Sue Urahn, and Abigail Zuger.

Additionally, we want to thank those family members who have listened to us for hours on end as we spoke about this venture: Ben Greene, Sandy Greene, Sue Kettl, Madeline Walter, and Wendy the dog.

Finally, a debt of gratitude is expressed to the people who were instrumental in making this book a reality: Stuart Krichevsky and Hannah Schwartz of the Stuart Krichevsky Literary Agency as well as Jon Sisk and Jaylene Perez of Rowman & Littlefield. Without the four of them, this book would still be little more than a good idea. With them, we hope, it is a collection of ideas that speak to us all.

Index

About the Authors

Katherine Barrett and Richard Greene are a husband-and-wife team who have been researching, analyzing, and writing about state and local government for over thirty years. They are columnists, senior advisers, and cochairs of the advisory board for Route Fifty; special project consultants for the Volcker Alliance; columnists and advisers for the Government Finance Officers Association; visiting fellows at the IBM Center for the Business of Government; senior advisers for the Government Finance Research Center; commentary editors for the International Journal for Public Administration; and fellows in the National Academy of Public Administration. For twenty years, until 2019, they were the management columnists for *Governing* magazine. Their most recent book was the *Promises and Pitfalls of Performance-Informed Management*, published by Rowman & Littlefield. Over their career they have also written about a number of nongovernmental topics, including two biographies and a documentary about Walt Disney.

Donald F. Kettl is professor emeritus and former dean at the University of Maryland School of Public Policy. Until his retirement, he was the Sid Richardson Professor at the Lyndon B. Johnson School of Public Affairs at the University of Texas at Austin. He is also a senior adviser at the Volcker Alliance, a nonresident senior fellow at the Brookings Institution, and a fellow of the National Academy of Public Administration.

Kettl is the author or editor of twenty-five books, including *Bridgebuilders: How Government Can Transcend Boundaries to Solve Big Problems* (with William D. Eggers, 2023); *The Politics of the Administrative Process* (9th edition, 2023); *The Divided States of America* (2020); and *Can Governments Earn Our Trust?* (2017). He has received six lifetime achievement awards, and three of his books have received national best-book awards. Kettl holds a PhD in political science from Yale University.